Family Council

Family Council

The Dreikurs Technique for putting an end to war between parents and children (and between children and children)

Dr. Rudolf Dreikurs
Shirley Gould
Dr. Raymond J. Corsini

Henry Regnery Company · Chicago

Library of Congress Cataloging in Publication Data

Dreikurs, Rudolf, 1897–1972
    Family council: the Dreikurs technique for putting
an end to war between parents and children (and between
children and children)

    Includes bibliography.
    1. Children—Management. 2. Parent and child.
I. Gould, Shirley, 1917- joint author. II. Corsini,
Raymond J., joint author. III. Title.
HQ769.D657   301.42'7   73-18183

Published by Henry Regnery Company
114 West Illinois Street, Chicago, Illinois 60610

Manufactured in the United States of America
Library of Congress Catalog Card Number: 73-18183
International Standard Book Number: 0-8092-9011-1 (cloth)
                      0-8092-9010-3 (paper)

For "Dr. D."
    In fulfillment of a promise.

                    R.C.
                    S.G.

Contents

Foreword

Dr. Rudolf Dreikurs died before the publication of this book. From the beginning of his career as a psychiatrist in Vienna in the 20s, he moved into the field of social psychiatry with an emphasis on education in the home and in the school.

He was an ardent proponent of the dignity of man as a self-determined and goal-directed being. He chose the vehicle of the psychology of Alfred Adler to teach and motivate people to work for a democratic society in which human equality, the dream of mankind, would come into being and bring with it peace and fulfillment for each individual.

He envisioned this democratic society not as a utopia but as a reality within reach. In Family Counseling Centers, workshops, and universities throughout the world, he emphasized the importance of the preparation of the child for future citizenship in a participatory democratic society.

The greatest potential for such preparation, in his view, was in the establishment of Family Councils in the home and group discussions in the classroom.

Unless the child, at the earliest age, experiences his own strength and a feeling of belonging, the opportunity for achieving the fullest measure of freedom with responsibility is lost. Once the child becomes a full partner in his family, the foundation of his future life is established, and he becomes a contributing member of his school and society. Man's potential can only be realized to its fullest when each human being is confident of his worth to the society in which he lives.

Dr. Dreikurs invited Dr. Corsini and Mrs. Gould to participate in preparing a book on how to conduct a Family Council. In this effort, he asked them to draw from their wide experience in working with families in education centers and in Mothers' Study Groups.

I wish to acknowledge gratefully the untiring and considerate efforts of Shirley Gould. It was she who visited and consulted with my late husband after the onset of his illness, thereby making it possible to complete this book.

It is my fervent desire that this book will serve to make the adventure of family living an exciting challenge, one that will lead to shared responsibility and equality in the home.

SADIE E. DREIKURS (MRS. RUDOLF DREIKURS)

Acknowledgments

The authors extend their appreciation to the families who furnished recordings and reports of their Family Councils for inclusion in this book.

1
Introduction

In our era of transition from autocratic to democratic relationships, parents are as ill-prepared to raise their offspring as their infants are to survive independently. But just as an infant, with the help of his family, overcomes his helplessness, so can the parents learn to become effective in raising their children.

The child, in trying to find a place in his family, uses alternative ways to reach his goals. In his creativity he can outwit his parents. They are no match for him and are unable to cope with and to guide him. When they become creative parents, they become better able to guide him. In this process, they need to understand the child and the goals of his behavior.

In the model of man advanced by Alfred Adler in his *Individual Psychology*, the child is seen as a self-determining person able to create his own style of life in the context of his family constellation. He is not a mechanistic product of his genetic endowment or his external environment; but through trial and error and his own observations, he forms his own conclusions about life and his place in it.

Every human being wants to belong, to experience his worth in a group. The first group for the child is his family. The child who is raised so that he experiences a sense of his worth to his family will have a sense of well-being and will behave in socially acceptable ways. The child raised in ways that prevent him from experiencing his worth as a member of the family group may employ useless means of finding a place in life, since he will become discouraged.

According to Adlerian psychology, all behavior is purposive. The basic striving for belonging and for social value of every individual has to be nurtured and cultivated.

The senior author has identified the four goals of the misbehaving child.[1] Such a child strives for a place in the family, but does so through mistaken goals, as follows:

1. *To gain attention*
2. *To demonstrate power*
3. *To punish or get even*
4. *To demonstrate inadequacy*

---

1. Rudolf Dreikurs, *The Challenge of Parenthood* (New York, 1948), p. 190.

1

In the family, the infant observes and interprets what he sees, hears, and senses about him, and begins at a very early age to create his personality—his character—through trial and error. The responses he receives from the people around him help him to figure out what his reaction can be. He is, generally, an acute observer but a poor interpreter.

In the family the child learns who he is, what the world is like, and how effective he can be in coping with it. From the way he is treated by parents, siblings, and others, he forms an opinion of himself that generally remains throughout his life. The family in which a child grows physically, whether his natural family, an adoptive family, a foster family, or even an institutional setting, is the laboratory in which the child works out his unique personality formula.

If the family is a competitive one, in which each member is constantly striving for superiority over the others, the child will decide that the world is a difficult place in which to survive, and that life is a series of tests and scores. Just as somebody always wins, somebody also loses; and he may decide he hasn't a chance to win. Or if he sees he can win, he may ever after be driven to prove he can win. Either way, he commits himself to a life lived in contest.

If, however, the family is a cooperative one, in which each member seeks to contribute to the well-being of the others while taking responsibility for his own behavior, the child may decide that he has a comfortable place in this kind of situation, and that the world is a place where he can belong.

A cooperative family atmosphere is the ideal toward which families ought to be working. Such an atmosphere is characteristic of a family in which children and adults treat one another with respect, in which each person has self-respect and a feeling of self-worth. Although some family members are bigger than others, some are older than others, and some are wiser than others, all treat one another as equal human beings with a worthwhile contribution to make.

In an atmosphere such as this, children can have confidence in their own abilities to grow, to develop, and to make good use of their natural endowments, whatever they may be.

To help achieve this atmosphere, we propose that families adopt the system of a Family Council. Working toward the establishment of an open democratic Family Council will assist everyone in reaching the kind of acceptance and feeling of belonging that breeds self-confidence and cooperation.

Human beings are in a constant state of movement, striving toward goals. With families, too, there is continual growth and movement. Perfection is not attainable. That is why we haven't included the script of an ideal family conducting a perfect Family Council. It doesn't exist. What we recommend is the activity of the search for equality, for democracy in the home.

Our advocacy of the Family Council is based on the following propositions:

1.   The Family Is an Organization.

It should operate in an orderly manner with a minimum of conflict. Each of the family members will prosper if he or she accepts the family's goals and objectives and if he contributes his share toward reaching for them. In families in which the members are friendly to one another, there will usually be found a high degree of efficiency. Each knows what he is to do, where the limits are, and how he can talk to the others. In these families there is open communication, cooperation, participation. By contrast, in families in which good feelings do not exist among the members, there will be found unequal and unfair division of labor, quarrels, misunderstandings, confusion, and general disorder.

2.   Emotions Follow Intellect and Behavior.

In general, people have to like one another before they can feel friendly toward one another; but this is not always true. A change in behavior affects the way people feel about one another, and it is quite possible to change a chaotic family—in which all are at war with one another—into a harmonious one, in which cooperation exists. What is necessary is a change in what each person does, and generally this starts with a change in one or both parents. How we feel about another person depends crucially on how that other person behaves toward us.

Many parents have discovered that staying out of children's fights has changed enemies into companions. For example, the Tompkins came for family counseling because they were exhausted trying to cope with the constant enmity between their two children, Margaret, 12, and Peter, 10. Although the children attended the same school, they had been sent to separate summer camps and in every way kept apart. Among other recommendations, the parents were advised to stay out of the fights completely.

Later Mrs. Tompkin reported that they had followed that advice, and took the risk of allowing both children to spend the summer at home. Not only did the fighting stop, but also with the beginning of school the children began to ride the bus together, regard each other as friends, and return at the end of the day engaged in animated conversation.

Now that Margaret and Peter have lost the need to compete for their mother's attention, they can allow themselves to love one another and to enjoy one another's company. By instituting a Family Council, their parents gave them a weekly forum in which they could participate, and helped them both to gain the valuable feeling of belonging to a viable organization.

The feelings that family members have for one another follow from the experience of how each one acts. If there is cooperation and mutual respect, warm feelings follow. If there is competition, quarreling, and belittling, hostile feelings will exist. That is: emotions are a function of behavior.

3.   Human Beings Can Function Only as Equals.

Only as equals can we function in a democracy. The idea that there is inborn goodness or badness in an individual has been discredited, as have many other superstitions, and we live by the declaration that "all men are created equal." To achieve a democratic relationship, there must be mutual respect; there can be no equality without it. If respect is desired in only one direction—that is, from children toward parents—there is no equality, for this assumes that one person is superior to the other. This is how parents teach children to try to win: to push the next fellow down, to minimize his achievements, to take advantage of every chance to win.

It is very difficult for most adults to accept a status of equality with their children. As long as parents are guarding their own superiority there can be no family harmony. Only when parents can admit to being fallible human beings, imperfect and willing to listen, will children begin to be respectful. A tyrant is to be feared and outmaneuvered, not respected. A democratic parent is seen not as an authority, but as a leader and teacher.

4.   Logic Works Better Than Force.

There are many ways parents try to get children to do what they want them to: bribery, threats, pleading, compulsion. Any one of those ways may work at the time, but each of them carries aftereffects.

If you bribe a child, you may find he will never do anything he doesn't want to do unless you can manage to give him a reward. This is hardly adequate preparation for adult life. How will he perform when there is no reward in sight?

If you threaten him, he soon learns to tell the difference between those threats you intend to keep and those that are empty, and to respond accordingly. The more a parent threatens, the more he has to eat his words, for children understand just how far they can go in the face of a threat.

If you plead with a child, you elevate him to the superior position and put yourself on your knees. No respect is earned, either for yourself or for him. And he will then go through life waiting to be begged.

Of course, someone who is bigger and stronger can always compel a smaller, weaker child to do his bidding. The aftereffect of force is stinging resentment, hostility bordering on hate, and a wish for revenge. The revenge may actually come at the same time: you can lead a horse to water, but you can't make him drink. You can force a child to scrub the floor, but you can't make him do it well. Nor can you prevent him from deliberately messing up something else.

In the Family Council, anything that affects family life can be discussed. When there is an open atmosphere, problems can be dealt with before they reach impossible proportions.

5.   Human Relationships Are Logical.

Just as society has expectations of parents, parents have expectations of children. The realities of maintaining life require that we live in society, among other human beings. Everybody is required to face the demands of life in interactions with other people. If parents attempt to protect their children from the world outside the family, they succeed only in crippling those children for the future. In the Family Council, through full participation and cooperation, younger members can learn to cope with the world outside the family. They can acquire the knowledge, the strength, and the courage to become active participants in the world around them.

As life goes on, there are consequences of every act—and of failure or refusal to act. Parents can take advantage of the continual interaction and movement of others by allowing children to experience for themselves the outcome of their behavior.

Each individual controls only his own movements, but influences the activities of others. When a parent understands this, he need no longer resort to autocratic measures, but can enter fully into the democratic interchange of a Family Council. Parents who understand the use of natural and logical consequences[2] need not fear to treat their children as equals.

6.   Parents and Children Are Engaged in a Cooperative Venture.

The family, although generated by parents, does not remain their sole responsibility. It belongs to all members, and each is required to make some contribution. From his place in the family a child first derives his feeling of belonging to society at large. To achieve the feeling of belonging, his contribution must be respected and he must get the message that he has value as a person. He is equal to others, but neither superior nor inferior to those he finds around him.

Many parents foolishly view themselves as having the sole responsibility for the family. They attempt to treat their children as honored guests to be shielded from life, to carry as little responsibility as possible.

These are the parents who exhaust themselves trying to be good to their children. They "know what's best" at all times, and try to be the ever-flowing fountain of gifts, wisdom, and experience for their children. Because children respond to such service and come to expect this treatment as their right, parents soon resent the demands of their children and begin to see them as their enemies. To triumph over them, they adopt countless ways to keep them down, to defeat them.

Children who are protected in this way are not equipped to deal with society, which is an interdependent organization.

As parents begin to see children as their equals, and to require from them cooperative contributions to the functions of the family, they will discover the benefits of democratic living together and find the Family Council an effective instrument to make this possible.

---

2. Rudolf Dreikurs and Loren Grey, *Logical Consequences: A New Approach to Discipline* (New York, 1968).

7.   Well-Being Depends on Cooperation.

Dreikurs's concept of the Family Council is derived from the theories of Alfred Adler, who held that man's fate in every respect depends on *Gemeinschaftsgefühl.* This German word is usually and inadequately translated as "social interest."[3] It is much more than that; it means a feeling for mankind, a concern for others, a social embedment, a solidarity with other human beings.

In contrast to some theoreticians who saw man as selfish, self-centered, aggressive, and hostile, Adler viewed man as a social creature for whom a sense of one's own worth and well-being depends on *Gemeinschaftsgefühl.* If children are not trained to be cooperative, they are being trained to be selfish, self-centered, and unhappy.

---

3. Alfred Adler, *Social Interest: A Challenge to Mankind* (New York, 1964).

2

What Is Family Council?

The Family Council is a way for family members to enjoy one another as people; a way to achieve mutual equality and respect.

A new dictionary says a council is either "an assembly of persons called together for consultation, deliberation, or discussion," or "a body of people elected or appointed to serve in an administrative, legislative, or advisory capacity," or "the discussion or deliberation that takes place in a council."

This is what we mean by a Family Council:

A group of people who live together, whether or not they are related by blood or marriage. The group shall have regularly scheduled meetings and operate under rules agreed upon in advance. The meeting shall be an open forum at which all family members can speak without interruption, with freedom of expression, without fear of consequences, and without regard for age or status. Its deliberations result in decision only when all members present agree—that is, come to a common understanding.

Since ancient times, human beings have known that life does not move along in a path of uninterrupted joy but that, from time to time, problems emerge that demand the best efforts of wise persons. In the councils of the church and in the councils of royalty, those who made the decisions were of superior status, divinely ordained. When their decisions were handed down, persons of lower classes had no choice but to obey. Modern municipal councils of elected representatives carry out the idea of deliberating on and deciding matters of importance to the entire community.

Today in our governments we strive for elected councils representative of all the people. When the councils make laws, they are supposed to enact the wishes of the people they represent. Citizens constantly try to get better communication between themselves and their elected representatives, so that legislation reflects the needs as well as the ideas of all.

7

Our history is full of declarations of equality, but actual equality is hard to achieve. It's hard to attain in the family too, but it can be done, with great rewards for all family members, parents as well as children. Everyone who participates in a Family Council can benefit from it.

In the effort to advise families how to live more happily and productively together, the senior author suggested the idea of *Familienrat* as one of the important means of achieving this. This word *Familienrat* means exactly "Family Council" in German, but there had never been a systematic method for conducting such a Family Council according to democratic principles.

There probably always have been some people who independently came to the idea of sitting down with the children and talking things over. But the Family Council is not merely getting together and talking. It is a whole apparatus for achieving democratic family participation in the solution of common problems and tasks.

In contrast to other kinds of councils, the Family Council is a joining together of equals. All members of the family are equal partners in the family, with functions and responsibilities according to their individual capabilities. They have equal status in expressing their ideas, their complaints, and their wishes.

Earlier writings of the senior author have expounded on the need for democracy in the family.[1] Here we will show that the Family Council is the single most effective device to help parents and children achieve the equality and democracy that will then assist them in solving the problems of daily living.

Learning to live as equals in a society that has not yet perfected the art of achieving equality is a big job for all members of the family. In order to learn this art, each person listens to the others, and all share in the responsibilities of family life, contributing not only their ideas toward the solution of problems, but also their daily efforts and activities toward the operation of the household.

It is not enough to trust to luck that there will be an opportunity for family members to talk to one another about their concerns. The family cannot just wait for such a chance. What works is the Family Council—a regularly scheduled meeting that everyone can rely on. Each one knows when it is coming. He can go about his daily business secure in the knowledge that there is not too long to wait for the next meeting, when he may air his problems, complaints, and suggestions. Besides, he knows that everyone will listen to him, which may not be likely at any other time.

No matter how difficult it is for parents to give up some of their authority, they are repaid when they realize that their children will listen to them. Children will cooperate, if given an honest opportunity on a continuing basis.

The continuation of the council is important, because at first it is difficult for children to believe that their parents really mean to treat them as equals, to listen to them, and to take their suggestions seriously. If parents keep on trusting the strength of the family in the Family Council, it will come to have a life of its own. The Family Council is not another in a long list of remedies for a family to try when all else has failed. It is a way of bringing together all family members to grapple with their mutual concerns. In order for it

---

1. Rudolf Dreikurs, "Raising Children in a Democracy," *Humanist* 18 (1958): 77–83.

to function effectively, it must continue through dull weeks as well as exciting weeks. The temptation may be great to skip a meeting now and then, and this is not a calamity; what is important is that parents not lose their trust in the concept.

For every family that wants efficiency and harmony, as well as for every individual who lives in close collaboration with others and wants to function fully and happily, it is essential to recognize social equality for all—expressed through shared responsibility in the Family Council. The unjust assumption of superiority of one person or one group over another is the basic cause for social conflicts, especially those of marriage and the family.

Equality does not mean similarity. It does not mean duplication. Equality does not mean that people are identical. Men and women are not alike, a baby is not the same as an adolescent, a child is not the same as an adult, and a foolish person is not the same as a wise one. There are many differences, but these differences should not confer high status and low status. Regardless of human differences in any relationship, equality exists through mutual respect.

When parents try to dictate on the basis of their assumed superiority through seniority, conflict erupts. It is just as dangerous for all concerned when parents are dominated by their children. The ideal toward which to strive is equality.

Children learn the rules of the game taught by their parents; if parents rule through power, children will seek to get some power of their own. If parents extend cooperation, children will learn cooperative ways.

Many parents talk things over with their children, but not in a systematic democratic way. The parents call it a discussion, but it is usually more like a court session in which the mother gives the report of the children's behavior, and the father decrees what should be done about it. Rather than an open discussion among equals, it is a lecture to which the children are obliged to listen.

When Adler originated the network of child guidance clinics, called *Erziehungsberatungstelle*, in the 20s and 30s, the public was not yet aware of an impending change in the attitudes of society. *Erziehungsberatungstelle* means literally "a place to come for questions about education"—a Parent Education Center.[2]

When Dreikurs brought the idea of Family Education Centers to the United States, and the idea grew and spread in the 50s and 60s, he advised families to set aside a regular time for a meeting with all members, so that everybody would have a regular chance to speak together. Actually, Dreikurs began the technique of the Family Council in Vienna, but elaborated on it later with his new experience in the United States.

The idea of a Family Council is not new, but we make a principle of it. We not only advocate the idea of a Family Council, but urge every family to create one. Clarifying how to do it and helping existing Family Councils to be more effective is the purpose of this book.

---

2. Rudolf Dreikurs, *The Challenge of Parenthood* (New York, 1948).

3

Explanation of Terms

In this chapter, in order to make the structure of the Family Council as clear as possible, we will explain the terms used in our definition on page 7.

Group of people. All the people living together, whether or not they are related, constitute the Family Council. This would include grandparents, aunts, uncles, cousins, the boarder, the guest who stays for the duration of more than one meeting—in short, anyone who is in close contact with family members, sharing the home. It is expected that, in most cases, the Family Council will consist of the parents and children, but the concept applies to other types of living arrangements. It may be used successfully, for instance, in a commune that consists entirely of members of one generation who are not related.

The aspects of living together that make a Family Council desirable for parents and children apply with equal force when additional persons are part of the household. In the modern commune, which seeks to experiment with new patterns of joint living, the technique of the Family Council is invaluable. Also, it is uniquely suitable in one-parent families.

Regularly scheduled meetings. It is of utmost importance that meetings be held regularly as agreed. Each family member needs to know just how long the interval is between meetings in order to understand how long he or she will have to wait to discuss a problem. For this reason, a specific time for the Family Council is to be scheduled in advance and clearly understood by everyone in the family. Thereafter, meetings are to be held at the scheduled times except in emergencies. Generally, a weekly meeting is preferable, but individual families may choose other arrangements. The time of day is not important, but it should be a period when all members are free for at least an hour, so that the family meeting will not conflict with other family functions.

11

The Family Council is not to be called only in an emergency, when there is an acute problem or a grave issue. In setting the time, it is usually successful to have meetings after a joint activity in which all participate—for instance, Saturday after lunch, Sunday after church, Monday evening after dinner, etc. It is crucial that no member needs to sacrifice any individual activity, or has to choose between that activity and the family meeting. The time of the meeting must be agreeable to all.

Rules. For the council to work well, there must be ground rules and guidelines. These should be discussed as soon as possible, to avoid having the early meetings get bogged down in arguments over procedures. Simple rules will do, although some families may rely on *Robert's Rules of Order,* especially if the family members are familiar with parliamentary procedure and feel comfortable with it.

One rule should provide for officers and how the offices are to be rotated. Generally it is desirable to have a chairman and a secretary, and to rotate these jobs on a planned system, including all children who are old enough to talk. The child who cannot yet write may appoint a helper, but it is important that children as well as adults take their turn at assuming the responsibility of office.

Open forum. In ancient Rome, this meant an open place for discussion, where any citizen could come and speak his mind. The Family Council serves the same purpose, giving every family member an opportunity to express his complaints, ideas, and opinions, and to hear those of the others.

If the sessions are used by parents just to repeat what they have been saying all the time and to tell their children what they ought to do, then it's not an open forum. For the Family Council to work, everybody has to have the chance to contribute, and every offering must be listened to with equal respect.

Without interruption. Each family member is guaranteed the chance to speak at any length. It is very trying, especially for parents, to sit and wait for a child to finish. It is equally trying for a child to listen to a familiar lecture from a parent. But this is necessary training for democratic procedures.

When somebody talks too much one must understand why. He wants to run the show, or be the boss, or be the center of attention, and he expects others to fight him. At this time it is necessary for the Family Council, in a noncondemning way, to discuss the goal of this disturbing behavior. When the person realizes that he does not provoke others, he will run dry. Incessant talking is like a temper tantrum, which does not go on without an audience.

Freedom of expression. There is absolute freedom of expression during the meeting of the Family Council. No topic, no language, no feelings are taboo. A child is not to be reproved for using gutter language, or for swearing. Neither is a parent nor a spouse to be chastised.

Why should a child be free to use insulting, vulgar, or accusatory language or to discuss ordinarily forbidden topics? We all use such language from time to time in other situations, in privacy, or with other adults. A child who uses such language in the Family Council may do so for some purpose that should be understood, not condemned. It may be used as a basis for discussion, but not for censorship.

Without fear of consequences. If there is to be absolute freedom of expression during the meeting of the Family Council, there must be a guarantee that punishment will not follow. The time during which the meeting is held is a "safety zone" protecting all members from the danger of retribution. Ideas, thoughts, and words which may be unsuitable at other times are to be allowed during council meetings.

Punishment is not part of democratic family life. It is only effective in an autocratic setting. We do have to teach our children proper morals and values, but punishment disregards human dignity, and is as such immoral. We all occasionally do things we know are not right; so do the children. But instead of punishing them and creating rebellion, we have to win them to accept what should be done, to behave as one should.

How will the child find out what it is that should be done? You can't just set the standards, because the child will no longer accept your standards. In the past the child had no choice but to obey. Today when you tell the child what your standards are, he may laugh. In most cases, when the child does something wrong he knows exactly what he should do, but he doesn't do it for a psychological reason. We have to help children see why they misbehave and help them to behave. It is the responsibility of parents to help their children understand why they did something wrong, and to help them want to do it a different way, a better way.

Fear of punishment has very little deterrent effect. It is more likely to create a wish for revenge. In holding a Family Council, we must realize that freedom of expression will not exist during the meeting if there is any fear of what will happen after the meeting.

Age or status. Regardless of age, all members must be treated equally. A child's contributions will be different, but his right to offer them is the same. Older persons undoubtedly have more life experience as well as more learned knowledge, but they do not have the right to impose their will on others. Neither should younger persons receive special consideration because of their youth.

If an idea offered by a young child becomes a family decision, even if it doesn't work out, the whole family can learn from it. Nothing is to be gained from parents' displaying their assumed superior judgment, but much is to be gained from treating a child's idea with respect.

Decision. When the group has grappled with a problem, the decision it makes can only be binding if every member present has given his agreement. If a unanimous decision is not reached, then every member has the right to do what he thinks best, but no decision that affects others is valid unless it has been approved by the Family Council.

Further problem solving is necessary to arrive at an agreement. Majority decisions lead to grievances by the minority and impede cooperation. Therefore, we caution against the use of voting in the Family Council.

Regardless of the content of the decision, it is most important that everybody have a chance to join in making it. The decision is not to be imposed by the adults; it is made by the children too.

In summary, in order for a Family Council to be effective, it must meet the following basic criteria:
1.   *Equality of all members*
2.   *Mutual respect*
3.   *Open communication*
4.   *Regularity*
5.   *Agreed rules*
6.   *Joint deliberation*
7.   *Reciprocal responsibility*
8.   *Mutual decision*

In addition to the gains made by parents in learning better ways of coping with their children, the children learn to express themselves, to be listened to, and to think independently about the concerns of the larger group.

4

Why Have Family Council?

The Family Council is a device, a technique, a procedure. What is most important in a family is the relationship among the members. This is why we urge families to have a Family Council: it is a prime means for improving that relationship, besides being a way to make the work of the family easier.

This is what a family wants and needs: an attitude of equality and mutual respect, a mood of helpfulness, a feeling of friendliness, an air of acceptance, and a spirit of kindliness. Instituting a Family Council and operating it by democratic principles is the way to attain all of these.

Each person in the family wants and needs each of these things, but is unable to gain them in isolation. Because of the social nature of man, every person requires interaction with others to gain a perception of his own worth.

The family represents to each individual a miniature of the world at large and, for the children especially, the patterns of living in the family determine how each person will conduct himself in relation to others. The personalities of the children are still forming and subject to change; but the adults can also discover themselves as interacting people, and retrain themselves toward more improved function in the outside world.

What follows will illustrate the way a Family Council can change family relationships from discord to harmony, from anger to hope, from discouragement to encouragement, and from indifference to involvement.

Most parents have a prejudice against their children, of which they are not aware. When it is pointed out to them, they will deny it. They express their love for their children, but don't realize how little and how poorly they show it. While they think they demonstrate parental love, they engage in intrusion upon, domination over, overprotection of, discrimination against, and manipulation of their children. The children then become angry, discouraged, resentful, and complaining, and they seek revenge.

15

In many families, relations have broken down completely. Undeclared war rages, complete with alliances, strategy, and heavy ammunition. Children, feeling mistreated, are wild and rebellious. The parents, feeling defeated, retaliate. Each sees only his own point of view.

Parents rail at their ungrateful children; children rail at their harsh lot in life. Every day begins with a fight to get the children out of bed and into their clothes, and ends with a fight to get the children out of their clothes and into bed. In between, there are battles about eating and playing, fighting and homework, a continuous war among people who love one another.

When children resent their parents and do not trust them, they are likely to have a secret and independent life, especially out of the home. They feel misunderstood, humiliated, bullied, managed, insulted, dominated, treated as incompetents. They see themselves as second-class citizens in the family, and rebel openly as soon as they are able.

When parents are confronted with open rebellion, they are often shocked and bewildered. Every parent wants a happy and harmonious family, and most mothers and fathers try hard to get it. Yet it often seems that those who do the most for their children have the most ungrateful children. They wonder what has "gotten into" their offspring, and are unable to realize their own contribution to the situation. It is easier to blame the current state of the world than to examine one's own share in creating it.

When parents pamper their children they do not realize how much harm they do. The child demands more and more, and the parents don't know what to do about it. They don't have any idea why the children behave as they do, so the parents try anything they can think of and only exacerbate the bad situation. They threaten and punish, and then weep, plead, and beg; but nothing works.

Because of the widespread condition of family warfare, parents regard it as a normal situation. It is a commonplace, usual, and expected condition.

What is the explanation for this tragic state? What is it that makes children resentful and suspicious of parents who are doing their best to prove their love for them?

Put as simply as possible, the underlying reason is the idea that parents are superior and entitled to boss. The culprit is the long-hallowed notion that father or mother knows best.

We are living in a new democratic society, in which nobody is willing to be dictated to. Children very early in their lives take it on themselves to do what they want and not what they are supposed to do. It is unfortunate that neither parents nor children have any conception of what they are really rebelling against. Nor have they any idea of how to call a halt to the rebellion and substitute a climate that will satisfy both generations.

When parents struggle to keep their own superiority, the battle is joined. The struggle between the generations that is fought on the apparent level of events and decisions is in reality a struggle of wills. This is a consequence of the democratic revolution in which everybody does what he wants. There always was a fight between the generations, but it never could come out in the open because society sided with the authorities. Today the rebellion of children begins very early in life and our children are continuously at war with adults.

Because present society is permissive and no longer sanctions punishment, parents have to learn to influence their children without fighting with them. Many parents abandon all effort toward achieving harmony because they have no idea how they can do it, but they can learn to exert influence instead of authority. The Family Council is one of the methods through which parents can do this.

In the continuing rebellion, parents become the slaves of the children. Children manipulate the parents, and the parents are not even aware of it. This begins while the child is still in the crib, when he learns he can summon his dutiful mother by a special kind of sound before he learns to speak any words. He quickly learns to put her in his service by faking legitimate need. As he grows, his list of maneuvers grows with him.

For example: Mother calls out to a small child, "Come in; it's too cold outside." Mother really believes it is too cold for her darling to be out; she doesn't believe her offspring has enough sense to come in out of the cold if he suffers. The child, feeling warm as he runs around in the snow, resents the command and wonders how his mother can be so dumb. Although she believes in her own superior wisdom and her responsibility to protect her child, the child experiences his own reality, one that is opposite to hers.

Even if this child were cold, he wouldn't admit it. He is determined to defeat her. The more the mother wants him to come in, the less likely he is to do so, regardless of how cold he gets. This is one way to defy her, to prove to her that she can't manipulate him, but that he can do what he wants.

In the past, when a child did something a parent disapproved of, he was spanked. He then gave up his bad behavior. Today, if a child does something wrong and you try to stop him, he only does something worse. He may do the same thing again in a different way, or find some other method to prove that he can have his own way.

This battle occurs on a thousand fronts. Parents say children are inexperienced, silly, immature, ignorant, weak, foolish—and need parental guidance and control. Children think parents are unfair, distrusting, nosy, picky, and overconcerned—and need to relax.

Who is correct? They both are; and there is the tragedy.

Toward a Solution

Such human conflicts are due to an inability to listen to one another. The Family Council is an artificial convention, a structure of relationships that helps young and old to communicate better and thus to understand one another better.

When parents feel desperate in their failure to control the family, they must learn to abdicate their role as rulers and arbiters and become guides and leaders. From laissez-faire or autocracy they must move toward participatory democracy, in which every individual has his full and equal role in the family.

Our solution is democracy in the family—equality in action. There is nothing wrong in a democracy that more democracy cannot cure.

What's in It for Me?

As you, the parent, learn from this book, you can achieve a more harmonious family. Changing a family is simple, but it isn't easy. It calls for an understanding of relationships in poor and in good families, and for an understanding of one's own actions, those of one's children, and the interactions of society. A good family is a work of art, but nobody has to be an artist to get it. You have to know what to do, and that is the purpose of this book.

Following are some of the benefits that accrue in a family that operates around the Family Council.

Happiness

Everybody wants to be happy. Many parents love their children but are unhappy with them. It isn't just the physical work connected with children that gets mothers and fathers down, but the irritations and frustrations that parents feel when they can't control their children's lives, behavior, and thoughts. Even though there is plenty of love, what is usually lacking is mutual respect. Parents expect children to respect them and other elders, but don't realize that children are equally worthy of respect. Happiness follows when mutual respect arrives.

Parents are quick to be offended when a child "talks back," and they demand that a child "show respect." But rarely does a parent stop and listen to himself as he talks to his child. The tone of voice tells the meaning. Often it communicates the message that the child is an inferior, inadequate, insufferable person who must do only as he is told.

The tone of voice a parent will use with another adult, a friend perhaps, is far more accepting, and carries with it the recognition of equality. Children hear these differences acutely, and rarely respond with respect when it is demanded. The way to elicit respect from a child is to treat him with respect so that he knows what it's like.

Very often when parents demand respect what they want is complete subservience. This is unattainable; and the attempt to get it leads to unhappiness. When there is mutual respect, there is harmony and, from that, happiness.

Efficiency

One of the consequences of equality in the family through the operation of the Family Council is that the business of the family can be done more quickly, more simply, and more efficiently. There are many tasks in every family, and several people who are capable of doing them. Some tasks are of an emergency nature and must be done at once. Some depend on the family's patterns of living and the kinds of activities they enjoy. But the bulk of the work in the household is for the maintenance of basic necessities: food, shelter, clothing, and education. It is of a constant, routine nature and must be done if the needs of family members are to be met.

The issue is who does the work and when. In most families the work is up to the parents, primarily the mother, who is considered to be the only one competent for the running of the household. Father is usually expected to furnish the sole financial support, and mother to do the housework. There is too little respect for the labor of the parents, and often mothers feel that slavery is the price of motherhood.

Thus the result is that children are lazy slobs, mothers are continuous cleaners, fathers expect total service; and there is in the household constant nagging, begging, and bickering—all because of the absence of democratic procedures.

The artificial notion is that father is at the top, mother a close second, and children below. In fact, father feels imposed upon and unappreciated, mother likewise, and the children keep busy trying to assert their independence in order to prove they are not on the bottom.

One of the functions of the Family Council is to explore the extent of the work load in the home, and to work at redistribution. The goal is more equality in responsibility and in mutual respect.

When the Family Council functions well, the work gets done without nagging and family members find new joy in the companionship of one another. All members develop competence in the performance of household duties. There is an exchange of onerous tasks so that no one person is perpetually stuck. Conversation between members becomes pleasant without bickering.

Communication

Will a Family Council increase or decrease the total amount of talking in the family? It may not do either; what it will do is improve the quality of the communication. Communication goes beyond words—we all know the impact of a look, a gesture, and how these can gladden or hurt. We are becoming aware of the meaning of other wordless communication as well: the message of a touch or the opposite message sent through putting oneself apart from others.

When the Family Council is functioning, most of the useless talk disappears: the reminding, complaining, nagging, scolding, and threatening are no longer needed. What do appear are the friendly conversation and the sharing of ideas that characterize relationships among equals. With mutual respect, children can risk reporting on situations they have experienced, even though they may not be shown in the best possible light. With mutual respect comes the courage to be imperfect, for parents as well as for children.

Most of us know that we're imperfect, but we spend our lives trying to be better than we are. Only when we can realize that perfection is unattainable can we cease reaching for it. Then we find the courage to be human, to be just good enough, imperfect persons in an imperfect world.

The person who is always striving toward perfection has to keep moving, and finds that he is not only moving up but sometimes moving down. He can never be sure that he is high enough, and therefore must live with tension, fears, and anxieties. He is constantly vulnerable.

The person who has the courage to be imperfect, on the other hand, need not be concerned with up or down, but can move ahead in the direction he chooses. If something goes wrong, he can try to find a way to remedy it, and does not need to worry about how his position has been affected. His prestige is not at stake, and therefore he is relieved of the necessity of preserving and protecting it.

Less Need for Punishment

Need for punishment diminishes as relationships among family members improve. Equals do not punish one another, neither do they reward one another. Behavior change will come about in children as they discover that they do not need to misbehave in order to get their parents' attention.

The speed of change in relationships depends on: (1) the ability of parents to understand the theory, the philosophy, and the practice of the Family Council; and (2) the readiness of parents to put this intellectual understanding into actual practice, with trust in the outcome and the emotional bravery to make the attempt.

The best training takes place when parents respect their children and create the atmosphere in which children want to respect their parents.

To illustrate what happens in a real family when the parents begin to understand the benefits to be derived from the Family Council, we quote from a long letter written by a mother about her own experience:

> My husband and I asked the children if they would be interested in trying a Family Council. The results have been as fascinating as they have been fantastic. We have all had to revamp our thinking and it has not been easy. We have had some setbacks that were learning experiences in themselves.
>
> There are six of us. My husband, Don, 31, is a carpenter; I'm 30, a housewife. Our children are Betty, 11½, sixth grade; Dick, 10; Janet, 7; and Roger, 6. We went into Family Councils rather hesitantly, with visions of each of our four children dictating to us. We were so wrong! We also had visions that this would be a big joke to them, and that they would really put us to a test to see how far we would go. We were wrong about that too.
>
> At our first meeting we set a few ground rules, the biggest one being that this was not a gripe session. We started with what has always been the biggest bone of contention at our house: bedtime.
>
> First we asked Betty what time she thought would be fair for her to retire, and to say why she thought so. She said ten o'clock because she is the oldest. Dick reminded us all that Betty never has to be called in the morning, that she always gets up by herself in plenty of time. The family voted, and she got the ten o'clock time. Dick was next. He said nine-thirty was a fine time for him, because Betty could then have the bathroom all to herself for a half hour. Janet was next, and said nine o'clock for her. Voted and passed. Then Roger said he'd like to stay up as late as Dick, but we disapproved. After discussion, we voted on eight-thirty and he agreed.
>
> By this time my husband and I were in a state of shock. We couldn't believe how serious our children were acting, and what good thinking they were using.
>
> At this first historic meeting, we also discussed chores. I had always given each child his chores each day, and then demanded that they do them, and watched until the chores got done. At the meeting, each of the children made a list of the chores they would agree to do for one week, and we discussed each list, changed some, and then agreed on them.

The first week was great. The children policed each other, and neither Don nor I had to say "Go to bed" even once. We only had to remind anyone to do chores twice all week.

The second week wasn't quite as good, but we were all learning. At the second meeting, I brought up the problem of the children forgetting their lunches, and told them that I would no longer bring them to school. Janet suggested that whoever forgot his or her lunch could charge lunch at school, but would have to pay for it out of his own money. We all agreed.

At the third meeting we all opened up a bit more. I accused them of not living up to their end of the deal, and they accused me of butting in too much. Don suggested it was time for a few more ground rules, and we agreed to have a chairman to preside at each meeting, rotating each week, so that each of us would have a regular turn to speak.

As we moved along from week to week, the time came when we had reached a standstill, and couldn't get agreement on the things that were bothering us. We suggested that we drop all agreements for a week and go back to the old ways to see how it would be. That whole week everybody was miserable. Don and I nagged, complained, hollered—everything we could think of, and nobody liked it. When meeting time came around again Tuesday night we started fresh, and I for one hope we never go through another week like that one.

Our whole family is learning to treat one another as equals, and I know if other families would try it they would get as much out of it as we have.

Sincerely,
Madge Cooke

Probably nothing the authors might say could strengthen the impact of those words. The letter is an eloquent answer to the question "What's in it for me?"

To understand the process through which this family has made gains, note that when Family Council began, it was the parents who made the move, in a somewhat autocratic manner. Yet at the end of the letter, this mother writes that she and all of them are learning. It is natural for parents to fumble at the beginning, to make many mistakes, and to feel as though they're not capable of participating in democratic family life. Nothing in their previous history or experience has given them the preparation for living as equals with their children. But every family can acquire the skills for solving conflicts and living cooperatively.

An accurate way to rate the conduct of a Family Council is to consider how you remember it. If you are a parent and you think "We decided," it is likely that one or both parents pushed through a decision without general agreement. However, if the meeting is recalled by "It was decided," it is much more likely that it was a mutual decision in which all family members reached agreement.

5

How Do We Do It?—Techniques

The techniques of holding a Family Council evolve from the principles that we have already stated. Briefly, it is to be a meeting of equals on a regular basis with the provisions set forth in the very beginning of this book.

When the adults in the family feel sufficiently informed about the purpose and the requirements of a Family Council, it is time for them to agree on starting it. Usually mother and father, having studied this book and at least one other of Dreikurs's books on the challenge of child-raising, discuss the necessity for a Family Council and how to have it in their own family.

Many of the parents with whom we are in contact are extremely hesitant about getting started. They are so anxious to do things the "right" way that they fear making a mistake. How you get started isn't as important as your attitude toward the whole idea.

If you falter and stumble, be assured that so has every other parent who ever tried to change his style of living with children. For most parents today, nothing in their background, training, or education has prepared them for an atmosphere of equality, or democratic family living.

Probably the most important attribute to have is one of openness. Think, "Let's see how can we go about this together?" rather than, "Now you're all going to come to the meeting I want."

1. Set the Date for the First Meeting.

When parents agree to begin a Family Council, they find a time for the first meeting when all the family members are able to attend. It is important that meetings be held on a planned basis, not just whenever someone gets a notion. Impromptu meetings carry with them the strain of impatience; usually they are called because of a conflict among family members when feelings are high, and calm discussion is impossible. Words in such an atmosphere become weapons, not communication. When the Family Council is operating on a regular basis, it is possible for the family to agree on procedures to be followed to cope with an unexpected situation.

2.   Invite the Others.

Parents inform all other family members of the decision to hold a Family Council, tell them the date and time the first meeting is to be held, and invite them to participate. At this point, children will ask many questions, especially if the family has not been operating democratically until this time. They will want to know, "What's in it for me?"—what kinds of decisions will be made and who will make them. They will probably also want to know what will happen if they decide not to attend.

There must be assurance that attendance is not compulsory, that anyone who wishes to absent himself may do so, but it is only fair to mention that decisions will be made regardless of the number of members who attend. This is not to be uttered as a threat, but rather as an explanation of what may happen.

3.   Include Everyone.

As stated earlier, every person who lives in the household is part of the Family Council, on an equal basis. In general, a child who can communicate with words is able to participate effectively in the Family Council. At the other end of the age scale, an elderly relative who lives in the home and seems to have little connection with the conduct of the lives of the younger generation is to be included in the Family Council and listened to with equal attention.

4.   Choose a Presiding Officer.

Each meeting needs someone to keep order; usually, he is called the chairman, although in some families other names are preferred, such as moderator, leader, etc. The office rotates on either a weekly or a monthly basis, so that every member has his chance to have the experience. Even though young children may not know how to perform in this responsibility, they learn by example. For this reason it is usually advisable for one of the adults to act as the presiding officer at the initial meeting, so that younger children get an idea of what needs to be said and done.

In whatever way this is decided, parents are to be especially careful not to issue instructions, but to allow all the children to express their opinions, ask questions, and decide together how the meeting is to be conducted and how the rotation is to operate.

5.   Give Information.

Before the work of the council meeting can begin, there should be a discussion of the way in which the Family Council will function. This is when parents tell what they have learned about equality in the family, and why they feel that a Family Council will be helpful to all family members. Questions will be asked about the outcome to which parents do not have answers. There must be honesty about this, so that the parents begin to demonstrate their willingness to abandon their authoritative autocratic roles. When children discover that their parents do not assume superior knowledge but can admit to some shortcomings, they will see the glimmer of the possibility for equality in the Family Council.

6.   Create the Ground Rules.

In order for the Family Council to function, the rules of operation must be acceptable to all. Some of the basic requirements have already been mentioned: the need for a regular time and place to meet; the need for a rotation system for officers; the need for unanimous decisions. In some families, more elaborate sets of rules, even going so far as a written constitution, may be developed, but the Family Council can operate effectively with only the few basic rules. As time goes on, circumstances may point to the desirability of additional rules to cover specific situations, but at the beginning, excessive discussion about ground rules can actually hinder the operation of the Family Council.

When the Family Council begins to meet, there will surely be difficulties to overcome. Unexpected subjects will come up and unexpected comments will be made as soon as the spirit of equality becomes evident. There is no way to predict what will happen, or how a family can cope with every situation, but the following are conditions to watch out for:

1.   Breach of Parliamentary Order.

In order for each member to have the right of free expression, every other member must listen to the one who speaks. Keeping order in a parliamentary manner enables the individual members to realize that everyone's turn comes in an orderly way. When a person wishes to speak, he is to be acknowledged by the chairman in his due turn. No one, especially not a parent, is to interrupt to correct, criticize, or expand on his comments. A parent may not use the session to preach, scold, or otherwise dominate the meeting, but may only express his opinion on an equal basis with everyone else.

2.   Emergency Decisions.

When a family member or even the entire family feels a state of crisis and is anxious for the Family Council to consider a problem, reasonable discussion is usually impossible. Most crises can stand a "cooling-off period" so that all family members can learn to tolerate an uncomfortable situation. The stronger the feeling in any one member that some decision must be made at once, the more likely it is that the better way would be to defer any decision. In the absence of a decision by the Family Council, each member is free to cope with the situation in his own way, but the consideration by all is often best delayed.

3.   Complaints and Nothing but Gripes.

Although the Family Council is an excellent forum for family members to bring up their problems and complaints about family living, it is not to be exclusively devoted to the airing of gripes and criticism. It is not a court to which everyone brings his hurts for judgment to be imposed, but rather the place to which everyone brings his problems in order for the entire group to deliberate on what they can do to help solve those problems.

Pleasant occupations can be brought into the Family Council by proposing the problem of how to have family recreation together—to bring before the group the decision about where to go on vacation, what outing to plan, what party to have.

4.   Wrong Decisions.

Often the children's inexperience will lead them to decisions that, in the light of the parent's greater experience, will appear to be in error. The temptation for parents to point out their superior wisdom is great, but unless the decision is life-threatening, it is more effective for parents to remain silent, and to allow the rest of the family to experience the results of such a decision. If the children discover for themselves how inappropriate their decision was, they will learn far more for the future than if they were to listen to one more speech about it from parents.

5.   Amendments and Alterations.

The decision once made must stand until the next meeting of the Family Council. No one has the right or the authority to change or alter a family decision between meetings. Nor does any member have the privilege of deciding on a different course of action and imposing his will on others. However, if some family members do not live up to the agreements reached at the family meeting, the others have the right to take appropriate action, or inaction. For example, if the children do not perform the chores agreed upon, the mother has the right not to perform those she agreed to do. If the dirty clothes aren't put in the right place, she can't wash them. If the kitchen isn't cleared as agreed, she can't prepare meals.

6.   Reciprocal Responsibilities.

No one person has the responsibility for the smooth functioning of the family—not the mother, nor the father, nor any one of the children. Just as all share in the equal privilege of addressing the meeting, and all share with equal voice in decision-making, all share in the responsibility for the total family, each according to his capability. Naturally father and mother will have a larger share of the responsibility, but it is important for mother to accept the distribution of labor and relinquish the burden of guilt if the family does not run as perfectly as she would like it.

When parents carry the total responsibility, children have no opportunity to learn to take care of themselves, much less shoulder other responsibilities. At the earliest age they must be considered worthy human beings who can cope with the requirements that life imposes on everyone.

7.   Pitfalls and Obstacles.

There are many ways in which a Family Council can founder. We have described only a very few of the most common. Others will become apparent in the rest of the book, where actual transcriptions of Family Councils appear, with comment. What family members must keep in mind is that the Family Council, when instituted, is a totally new and untried device for family functioning, and it will require time and effort before it can succeed. The operation of a Family Council requires cooperation on the part of all. It requires a shift in roles by all members of the family, and presents new challenges to everyone who participates. In the competitive society in which we live, cooperation is hard to achieve, but it can develop.

It cannot be expected that a group of people living together will function smoothly as a unit all the time. There will be friction, there will be conflict, and at times it may seem that it takes too much effort to keep the Family Council going. In the long run every member of the family will grow and be strengthened through the continuing effort to learn to live as equals. Even if no meeting takes place for a period of time, it is worthwhile to start up again. The next time the council may work better, and each time it is possible to accomplish something. Even a small gain is worth working for.

6

Getting Started

In the preparation of this book, the authors have had the cooperation of many families who recorded their Family Council meetings in order that others could profit from their errors and their successes. The material that follows has been extracted from those recordings, with the names of the participants changed in order to preserve their anonymity. The comments that accompany each excerpt are intended to illuminate the difficulties to be encountered when people try to find the democratic way of equality. They are in no way to be interpreted as criticisms of the parents, or of the way they speak. Each of the families whose meetings are quoted is in the process of learning. The purpose of the comments is to assist everyone in grasping the ideas in order to learn by example.

When sections follow one another, it is because the particular problem, or the subject matter, is related, and not because this is the way it really developed in any one family. The difficulties are universal, and each family can learn something by studying the experience of another. The subject matter varies according to many factors: the age of the children, the size of the family, the living arrangements, to suggest just a few. However, the challenge is constant: to learn to live democratically, to experience equality in action.

After Ross and Alice, parents of two daughters, a preschooler and an infant, decided they would like to hold a Family Council, it was difficult to figure out a way to explain their idea to their young child. They just seized the opportunity when all three were together, talking about an important problem.

Lois, the preschooler, was concerned about going to the dentist:

LOIS: Mom, when are you taking me to the dentist?
MOTHER: Is that what you want to talk about? Tell me about it. Shall I make an appointment for you?
LOIS: Yes.
MOTHER: And you'll go with me to the dentist, and what'll we do there?

LOIS: He'll have to fix the hole in my teeth.
MOTHER: You have a hole in your teeth?

Neither mother nor father is satisfied that Lois understands the planning, and both err in trying to make a heavier impression.

FATHER: Tell me something. Why do you have to go to the dentist?
LOIS: 'Cause I have a hole in my teeth.
FATHER: Oh.

Without much practice in conversing with their daughter as equals, both parents show the overconcern that most parents have: their anxiety to make sure comes through in the way they shower her with words. They ask the same question repeatedly, and give the same answers.

MOTHER: OK, you know this week mommy has to go back to her dentist downtown; so you're going to stay with Aunt Hope again while I go to the dentist, 'cause he found another hole in my tooth, and I have to go have it filled. Then, one day next week—should we make it next week, or when would you like to go to the dentist?
LOIS: Today.

Mother started by telling, and ended up by asking. In attempting to give Lois a choice, she drew an unexpected answer.

MOTHER: Well, I can't get an appointment today, because it's too late, but shall I call him and ask him when we can come?
LOIS: Yeah.
MOTHER: OK. The same dentist Sue goes to?
LOIS: No.
MOTHER: Why not?
LOIS: The same one you go to.

Lois's perception of the dentist is apparently different from her mother's. Since mother spoke of her own relationship to a dentist, it was natural for Lois to assume that she would go to the same one. Mother has a different idea, and in attempting to explain the difference, launches a sales talk, in which father joins, to overpower her with words. Note Lois's natural response.

MOTHER: The same one I go to? The one I go to is just for mommies and daddies and adults, and I want you to go to a dentist that's for children. He'll give you your very own toothbrush. He's got little things for you.

FATHER: How does that sound? Pretty good, huh?

Father not only joins in the promise of a reward, but gives Lois the words he expects to hear.

LOIS: I've got a blue and a pink toothbrush. The baby could have my blue tooth-brush, because she likes blue.
MOTHER: Yes, maybe.
LOIS: Now we all stand up and . . .
MOTHER: What, honey?
LOIS: I want to play "Simon says" and you all got to do what I say.

Lois knows the subject is closed, that mother will make the arrangements. Perhaps in answer to her parents' power over her, she wants to play the game where she will be in power. But her parents aren't ready.

MOTHER: But we're having our Family Council right now.
FATHER: We're having Family Council.
MOTHER: Maybe afterwards.
LOIS: Then I'll play "Simon says" by myself, and I'll be Simon. 'Cause I was the first.
MOTHER: Is there anything else you want to talk about? You brought up the dentist. Is there anything else you want to talk about?
LOIS: That's all. You do the rest.

This would have been an excellent time to finish up, but the parents in their eagerness keep the meeting going for a while longer. Lois has lost interest, but they manage to involve her a few more times.

MOTHER: OK. We'll try doing that this coming week. We'll see what happens.
LOIS: Now let's play "Simon says."
MOTHER: All right. I suppose we can play "Simon says" now.
LOIS: Simon says, "Stand up!"
MOTHER: Are we finished with our Family Council?
FATHER: The end. Right?
MOTHER: Shall we have another one next week? Let me just tell you one more thing about our Family Council, and then we'll be all done. If you have something that you don't like, or something that you might be angry about, or if daddy or mommy have something that we're angry about, or if we have something that we really ought to know and that we'd like to talk about, we remember it—you remember it, and you save it, and next time we have a Family Council, you'll tell me all about it. OK?
LOIS: Simon says, "Stand up!"

Mother slipped, saying "You'll tell *me*," but her intentions are good. She kept talking, but her daughter stopped listening. Lois has been trying to play her game for several minutes, and probably tuned her mother out. What is valuable is the spirit that has begun to take shape. The parents finish the meeting, join in the game, and demonstrate to Lois that her wishes are important too, and that they can all have fun together, enjoying one another.

In a family where the oldest child is quite young, this is an excellent approach. Before you invite the child to participate in the first Family Council meeting, be aware of a situation about which you can ask the child's opinion—and be prepared to give that opinion as much consideration as your own.

Suitable examples would include minor decisions that include the whole family, such as where to go for a weekend outing, whom to invite to a child's birthday celebration, or how to arrange the space for the expected arrival of a baby. Neither the child nor one adult is to have the absolute decision, but the opportunity is opened for joint discussion, and the expressed ideas of a young child can be surprisingly fruitful.

With very young children, one needs to be very careful not to "talk down." Young children as well as older ones respond better to the tone of voice that communicates respect than to the tone that says you marvel at and admire their littleness.

In another family, the children were older when the parents decided to try a Family Council. With two sons, Brad, age 17, and Skip, age 9, father felt a thorough explanation was in order and delivered an opening lecture:

FATHER: This is our first Family Council. I guess we ought to define what a Family Council is and why it is. The Family Council—you can call it anything you like—is like a board of directors or something like that in a corporation. You have to have people in the company look after the company and report to the company in periodic sessions to orient themselves on the direction of the company and determine which way to go, or how it's going to go, and what its accomplishments are, what its objectives are supposed to be, and how to go about accomplishing the objectives.

Well, this could be our little board of directors. We have a corporation, that is to say, the family, and if we want to accomplish things, we have to sit down together and establish objectives and how we're going to go about achieving them. This is one technique—the Family Council—that we can use to do that.

I suppose our purpose in being here right this minute is to see if we can establish a kind of council or board of directors and to make it mean something to the improvement of our lives and the life of the family. Whatever it is we do, we want to make sure that we have some kind of record so that we don't forget what we decide or do not decide to do about various things, so that there be no mistake as to what we're going to do or how it's done. Skip has decided that he would like to try to be the secretary. It's the secretary's job to take the minutes and to keep records of decisions that are made at each meeting. Does anybody have any questions as to purpose or anything?

Here we have a demonstration of an over-anxious father, so concerned to make his explanations that he is guilty of too much talking and too much selling. The entire tone of his speech is condescending, as though only he could explain to the others. He is probably a very diligent father, wanting to do his job well, but he does not respect the ability of the other family members to grasp his meaning. This is an example of very good intentions carried so far that the results might have been poor, as well as a warning to other parents to avoid this trap.

This father learned how to be less pedantic. Three years after their first meeting, with the older son now in college and the younger entering adolescence, the family still meets regularly in a Family Council and has learned to deal with its problems together in a democratic manner.

The meeting continued with a discussion about who would do what:

SKIP: Well, if dad and I are supposed to do jobs—if dad is chairman and I'm the secretary, what can the other two be?

This question shows a misunderstanding of the concept of equal participation in the meeting. They went on to discuss at length a system for rotating the two necessary officers, with Skip taking an active part in the discussion. Finally, father as chairman, summed up:

FATHER: We only at this moment have chairman and secretary. That's not necessarily all that there can be, but that's all we have right now. Tomorrow or next year it might be something else, but right now, at any rate, Brad has suggested that we rotate the jobs every week.

SKIP: Right. Will anyone second the motion?

FATHER: Are there any comments on this?

SKIP: Anybody want to second the motion?

FATHER: Any comments on the jobs? Does everyone agree that we should rotate the jobs every week?

MOTHER: It's fine with me.

FATHER: We'll have a new chairman and a new secretary every week.

BRAD: A new chairman and a new secretary next week?

MOTHER: Yes, rotate every week.

SKIP: You're the chairman.

MOTHER: Wait a minute, dear, we do this by agreement.

SKIP: Oh.

MOTHER: Shall we go clockwise, or counterclockwise?

BRAD: We ought to have it orderly.

SKIP: But it can't be voluntary, because if nobody volunteers, you're left without a chairman. I put it down in the minutes so that we know what we're supposed to do. Next week, mother is chairman, then Brad, then me. Then in the next column I have secretary next week, Brad, then dad, then mother.

MOTHER: Why don't we just rotate clockwise around the table?

BRAD: How about clockwise for chairman and counterclockwise for secretary? That'll work.

Having agreed on a method for sharing the responsibilities of the Family Council, this family went ahead to discuss plans for a summer trip, but made no final decisions. Before adjournment, father again made a few long speeches about future meetings. There was discussion about the time for future meetings, and the length of each meeting.

FATHER: As we're starting these Family Councils, we don't know exactly how to handle them, how to respond, when to stop interrupting one another, and how to arrive at a quick effective decision. We're liable to talk a subject to death, and probably it'd be a pretty good idea, at least in the beginning, to have a time limit on the meetings. I do think as we get more accustomed to the meetings, we will have a little more to say. We'll have a better idea of how they should be carried on, and the meetings will probably time themselves. We'll probably have a purpose, an objective, and we'll discuss it effectively, and we'll arrive at a decision, and that'll be it. But in the beginning, I don't think it'll be easy, so I think we ought to have a time limit, at least for the first half a dozen meetings.

BRAD: I move that it be a half hour.

MOTHER: I think we ought to have a set time to start, also. I think if we have something else to do . . .

SKIP: After lunch.

BRAD: Yes, after lunch. Whenever we're finished with lunch.

MOTHER: Well, what happens, for example—next week I'm going to be doing something for the Boy Scouts after church, so it'll take me longer. I'll have to clean up the mess and everything, so it might be twelve-thirty before I get home.

BRAD: We don't have to be so prompt on Sunday.

MOTHER: But if we make a time for our meeting, we can work around it.

SKIP: Twelve-thirty.

BRAD: No later than one o'clock.

MOTHER: We can start earlier, right?

FATHER: No later than one o'clock. We may start earlier. We'll meet for a half hour, till one-thirty. Got it?

SKIP: Right.

MOTHER: Everything is tabled until next week, right?

FATHER: OK, the meeting is adjourned.

7

Planning the Procedure

Suppose you want to start a Family Council now. You have the general idea of open communication on an equal basis, and the whole family has talked about doing it, but you wonder if there's a special way to proceed. There are many ways, and each family must find the one that suits it while adhering to the general principles described in earlier chapters.

If you have any experience with formal meetings, you have a general idea of how they move. You may take anything from that procedure that you feel fits your family. Some families merely bring up "old business" and "new business," making sure that each member has a chance to be heard.

Another outline is:

1. *Household jobs*
2. *Things that have shown improvement*
3. *Things that need improvement*
4. *New business*

With any procedure, it is essential that the basic principles of equality and open listening prevail. However, an attempt to hold a Family Council meeting without any structure may result in chaos. Without leadership and without a plan, everybody may talk at once about anything that comes to mind, with the result that no one listens to anyone else. If there is an outline of procedure for the meeting, and if family members are familiar with the outline, it is much more likely that fruitful discussion will take place.

The major caution we stress is to avoid taking votes. Majority rule may be effective in government, but if the majority wins in the family, the minority will surely find ways to make the decision ineffective. If unanimous agreement does not emerge naturally from discussion, it is best not to demand a vote. In the absence of unanimity, the family can agree to postpone the decision until the next meeting, or to drop the subject from consideration.

The danger in majority rule is that the more powerful members of the family (whether parents or children) actually push through their viewpoint against the wishes of the others. This activity breeds resentment through competition rather than harmony through cooperation.

In the Gould household, the agenda for the meeting has these six items:

1. *Minutes of the previous meeting.*
2. *Banking (treasurer's report)—allowances and other financial transactions between parents and children: deposits, withdrawals. Decisions about money come later in the meeting.*
3. *Calendar for the coming week. Discussion of individual dates, transportation, baby-sitting, and mealtimes.*
4. *Old business.*
5. *New business.*
6. *Future plans, especially for fun together.*

Still another informal way to begin a Family Council meeting is for the chairman of the day to ask the others, "Any reaction to last week's meeting?" The responses to that question will offer subjects for discussion at the current meeting. These topics should be listed by the secretary, to be taken up later in the meeting. Then the chairman may ask, "Any reports on the past week's decisions?" Answers to this question will demonstrate to the family how well things have worked out. It is possible that earlier decisions may not have proved workable. It is also possible that a subject that was too controversial to be handled last week has cooled off enough during the week so that it can be tackled now.

These two questions are roughly equivalent to the business of the meeting.

It is helpful to know what parliamentary rules are. You may wish to refer to the simplified rules that follow to help settle arguments that may erupt over how the Family Council is supposed to operate. It is always better to let an impartial rule make the decision, and thus avoid a wrangle over who knows better.

Orderly Procedure
Based on Parliamentary Rules

ORDER OF BUSINESS

1. *Meeting called to order by chairman*
2. *Minutes of preceding meeting read by secretary*
   a. *May be approved as read*
   b. *May be approved with additions or corrections*
3. *Report of treasurer*
4. *Unfinished business called for, either by chairman or by others*
5. *New business called for by chairman*
6. *Motion to adjourn*

DUTIES OF CHAIRMAN

1. *Preside at the meeting*
2. *Keep calm at all times*
3. *Talk no more than necessary while presiding*
4. *Conduct the meeting in a businesslike manner*
5. *Extend every courtesy to those present*
6. *Always appear a few minutes before the time of the meeting*

DUTIES OF SECRETARY

1. *Write any letters that the group may designate*
2. *Keep a neat and careful record of all business done in the meeting, noting always what is decided and not just what is said*
3. *The minutes should contain*
    a. *The date and time of the meeting*
    b. *All motions made and decisions arrived at*

DIFFERENT TYPES OF MOTIONS

Note: When a motion has been made and seconded, the group may not consider any other business until this motion has been disposed of. All important motions should be seconded by someone other than the person making the motion.

1. To amend: *To change, add to, or remove words from the original motion.*
2. To table: *To postpone the subject under discussion in such a way that it can be taken up at some time in the future.*
3. To postpone: *Similar to table; may be put off for a longer time.*
4. To reconsider: *To take up something previously passed, and have new discussion about it.*
5. To move the previous question: *A way to close debate when discussion becomes drawn out; a request that the group come to a decision.*
6. To adjourn: *The official way to end a meeting; one person makes the motion, the others agree.*

The Harris family keeps a journal in which members take turns recording the decisions made at each meeting. Just as the chairmanship rotates, so does the record-keeping. Once, when they started to disagree over what they had decided before, they looked it up in the journal. (At this meeting, Jeff, age 6½, was chairman, and mother was secretary. There are two other brothers: Ken is 11; Larry, 9).

KEN: Well, is this the end of the subject?
MOTHER: No, I made a suggestion that I don't think it's up to dad to have to replace.

LARRY: Well, since we got our allowance raised, remember we said it'll be used to buy supplies for us?

FATHER: Your own clothes and things like that?

LARRY: Yeah.

KEN: I ain't going to buy my own clothes with a dollar a week.

LARRY: You could go back to the . . .

MOTHER: That was just pertaining to socks and I think if we check in the journal on the back pages it was—no one agreed on that.

LARRY: Then we should have our allowance back down.

MOTHER: That's not really why—excuse me.

JEFF: Mom?

MOTHER: That's not why the allowances were raised. If you read back in the journal, Larry, I think you'll see that they were raised because it was difficult for you to buy school supplies and things like that and replace pencils . . .

LARRY: And socks.

MOTHER: Excuse me. Better call on somebody else, Jeff, and I'll see if I can find it.

KEN: Jeff, can I bring up a new subject?

MOTHER: Are you talking to me?

JEFF: Mom, are we finished with that one?

MOTHER: I'm looking it up in the journal, OK?

KEN: Jeff, we can go back to that one. I want to bring up a new subject.

After a long discussion about privacy, and whether Ken should be able to come into Jeff and Larry's room, mother found the reference to allowances in the journal:

FATHER: I think we spent enough time on the rooms and we still haven't reached a solution. Mom's found the part about the allowances, so let's hear it.

Note that Jeff, age 6½, is chairman of this meeting, but father assumes the responsibility for moving it along. Mother is secretary, but in this instance it sounds as if both parents are simply taking over the meeting and running it. This is one of the most common errors that parents can make, and is often the reason why children lose interest in coming to a Family Council.

MOTHER: All right. This is from March 31st when your allowances were raised. I brought up the fact that I would like to know how they feel about raises in the allowances, and if this should include taking care of school supplies, socks, etc. Dad agreed to raise allowances: Ken to get $1; Larry, 75¢; and Jeff, 35¢. We had a big discussion about it, and it's all in here, and no one agreed that this should include socks; but it was also agreed that parents do not have to replace clothing, including socks, because of carelessness. If dad is responsible for paying for it, and you kids are careless, then he doesn't have to.

The Harris family keeps very detailed records, but there are also simple ways. If a notebook is provided, it is only necessary to record the date and the main decisions made. What is important is that there is an impartial record to be referred to in case of a dispute. This alone helps to keep down arguments so that everybody can deal with the business of the present.

What if there are no problems when the time comes around for Family Council? This can happen, but it's a good idea to hold the meeting at the regular time anyway. When the family is assembled, someone may spontaneously remember something he or she wanted to bring up; or an idea may emerge that will produce joy for everyone. Especially as the children get older, this may be the one certain time during the week when everybody is together.

You can't just sit and look at one another. If the family gets in the habit of following an agenda, going over the calendar for the week, and reviewing job performance, there will always be a few things to get the discussion going.

It is also wise, when making new plans, to make them for just one week. At the end of the trial period everyone can discuss how that plan worked and decide together whether to keep it going, or to try another way.

The family in the following excerpt had been discussing whether or not they could go on a company outing to see a baseball game. The cost for each person would be $6, and they were trying to decide whether the trip and the reserved seat would be worth that much money. There were many reasons in favor, and just as many against, so before any hostility could come to the surface, mother suggested:

MOTHER: How do you feel about postponing any decision until next week? We can talk about it among ourselves in the meantime, and then decide at the meeting. Will that still be enough time? That's the eleventh.

FATHER: We can pick up tickets until the fifteenth.

Thus an argument was avoided, and each person had an opportunity to think over the idea before any final decision was made. Postponing the decision for a week didn't harm the chances of going ahead with it. On the other hand, a week later the whole idea might not be so inviting, and it might be discarded. Most important, nobody could get railroaded into going along with the others if he didn't feel like it.

In another family, mother brought up her distress about a mess around the front door:

MOTHER: There's no vestibule here, and when your feet are wet or muddy and you come through the front door, you get some dirt on the white floor. If you go to the back, you get the mud on the floor by the kitchen, and the front of the house stays nice.

DAVID: But other people come in the front door. They might have mud on their shoes. Would you say "Go around to the back" to them?

GAIL: And the same thing for you or daddy.

MOTHER: You mean guests?

GAIL: Right. And they may have muddier feet than we do.

DAVID: Yeah—they might by accident have mud all over them.

FATHER: I think we might be able to solve part of the problem by putting a piece of carpet down there to wipe our feet on.

DAVID: Until they get clean.

GAIL: I think we can take off our shoes.

MOTHER: All right, I'll tell you what. I'll be willing to try it for one week, and we'll discuss it next week if it seems to be a problem. Is that OK with everybody?

Mother, meeting opposition to her request, understands that what is especially important to her conflicts with the wishes of the rest of the family. Rather than pressing the issue, she has agreed to put the subject off for one week and bring it up again. She hasn't said what she's going to try, but in the meantime, each family member will be aware of mother's wishes. The next time the subject comes up, it can be discussed with the experience in mind. There doesn't need to be a contest over whether mother is right, and whether she should get her way. She has expressed her wish, and the subject is and will be treated with respect.

There are very few decisions that can't be postponed for a week; likewise, there are very few solutions that can't be tried for at least a week. When everyone agrees that they'll see how it works out, everyone will be watching and paying attention. Then when it comes up again, there is something to talk about.

On the question of performing one's household tasks, children may ask to be reminded. Parents don't want to be policemen, and feel that children should take the responsibility for remembering their own contributions to the household as well as remembering the things that suit their selfish purposes.

Rather than refusing to do any reminding at all, this father felt it would be all right. The mother clearly did not:

FATHER: Well, they don't ask to be reminded all the time, just once in a while; so why don't you try it just once in a while, and we'll see how it works out?

MOTHER: All right. What happens in between then?

FATHER: We can discuss it next week if it doesn't work out.

Father doesn't realize that what he has done is to put the burden on mother for something she doesn't want to do. Mother is appropriately reluctant to remind the children to do the jobs they have undertaken to perform. She doesn't need to carry the burden of telling them, but father feels she should go along with the children's request. Next week, at the family meeting, if mother wishes she can report how many times it was necessary, and thus make her point that the responsibility has remained on her rather than on the children, where it belongs. What is missing in the conversation is the participation of the children.

Dialogue between father and mother appears to keep them both in charge, ignoring the possibility of shifts in the children's viewpoint. Instead of a discussion in which all members of the family join, there is a disagreement between the parents. However, by agreeing to bring it up next week, they have avoided a fight over their disagreement, and allowed for a reasonable approach to the subject when it comes up again.

Sometimes the same subject may come up every week for many weeks. It doesn't matter, as long as different approaches are tried. Everybody will learn something each time, without getting into conflict over opposing views. Without any authority to pronounce a decree, each family member will feel that his opinion is worthwhile. Each one will earn the respect of the others and in turn respect the opinions of others.

Each person views family life from his or her own perspective, and it is likely that each will have a different opinion about something. Sometimes two or more people join to oppose another, just for the sake of trying to win. When the decision is postponed, however, nobody loses and everybody wins, with the end result that a decision is finally reached that everyone can accept. Each one is free to move away from his original position toward agreement with the others.

The following excerpt is a verbatim transcript of a meeting of the Curtis family, which consists of the parents and two sons: Mike, age 10, and Ed, age 7. The parents have been studying Dreikurs's principles for three years, and have been holding a Family Council for two years. In this meeting, they were continuing a discussion about how to find solutions to a family problem:

ED:	I want to bring up what you started.
MIKE:	What's that?
ED:	Being left out in the back room.
MIKE:	He just said a problem. Now if we would all say . . .
FATHER:	Shall we clarify the problem?
MIKE:	Ed does not like to be left out in the back room at night.
MOTHER:	You don't either, Mike.
FATHER:	You mean when you fellows fall asleep on the floor, or on the couch, and mother and I go to bed and leave you lying there, you don't like that?
MIKE:	Right.
MOTHER:	Have you any ideas?
MIKE:	If you would just say to yourself, if dad would just say to himself, "Well, I'm going to wake Ed up just once before I go to bed. . ."
FATHER:	That's a possibility.
MOTHER:	Can we put that down as one solution?
MIKE:	Right.
MOTHER:	Wake up . . .
MIKE:	Before going to bed, wake up Ed once.
MOTHER:	OK, wake up person once. Have you any other ideas? Ed, have you any suggestions?

ED: We wouldn't really have this problem if the bedtime was established and we stuck to it.

MOTHER: That's true. I'll put down "Establish bedtime."

ED: Unless it's the day before Saturday. Bedtime when there's a holiday would be nine o'clock.

MOTHER: That's one of the solutions. We can discuss all of the solutions later.

MIKE: All right.

MOTHER: Any other ideas?

MIKE: Any other subjects?

MOTHER: We're not finished with this one.

MIKE: Are there any more solutions?

FATHER: How about if we don't allow blankets or pillows to be used?

MIKE: No, that's not a practical solution.

MOTHER: We can always rule it out later.

MIKE: No, but you see . . .

FATHER: The reason I'm saying this is because you get too comfortable, and you fall asleep.

MIKE: But these rules I just brought up.

MOTHER: These are not rules. These are only suggestions . . .

MIKE: But if you say to yourself in your mind, "I'm going to wake him up one time," you don't need to write it down or anything. You just say that to yourself.

MOTHER: That's not what we're trying to do. You don't understand.

MIKE: I do understand, but I don't want to have a long meeting time. I brought that up to shorten the meeting, so we have more time to do other things. Now, bringing up a solution like "no blankets or pillows" is going to go on for thirty minutes.

Although the rest of the family is working toward a system for reaching solutions to problems, Mike, who has been accustomed to getting his own way, feels that he has the perfect solution, and wants everybody else to agree with him. The parents, with some patience, attempt to explain:

MOTHER: We just put it down on paper and accept it or reject it as the best of all possible solutions.

MIKE: Reject it.

ED: I'm not going to stay.

FATHER: Wait till we get all possible solutions and then we'll decide which one you would like to try for a week.

There remains disagreement about what solution would be acceptable to all:

MIKE: Let me read the list of possibilities. "Wake up person once." Who thinks that would be a good . . .

MOTHER: What are the other alternatives?

MIKE: "Establish a bedtime. No blankets or pillows allowed."

MOTHER: I would like to scratch that one out.

MIKE: All right. Number three is scratched.

FATHER: Why? We haven't all agreed to it. Mother wants to scratch it out. Maybe I don't want to.

ED: I agree to it.

MIKE: Well, I want to scratch it out.

ED: What is number three? No blankets?

MIKE: No blankets.

ED: I scratch it out.

MOTHER: I don't think having blankets is the problem.

FATHER: Sure. They get too comfortable. If they had to sit up in a hard chair, they wouldn't fall asleep.

MIKE: No.

FATHER: All right. You can scratch it.

MIKE: All right. The others are: "Wake up a person once"; and "Establish a bedtime."

ED: I don't want to scratch it.

MOTHER: Maybe we could use those last two suggestions in conjunction with each other.

ED: How?

MIKE: Set a bedtime, like nine o'clock, or nine-thirty, and if the person falls asleep, you wake him up just once at the bedtime, and if he doesn't get up, then you let him lie there.

MOTHER: What do you think of that?

MIKE: That's good.

ED: That's good.

FATHER: I don't like it.

MIKE: Why not?

MOTHER: Do you have another suggestion?

FATHER: I like the second one, where we establish a bedtime; the boys are old enough to know that when it's eight-thirty or nine o'clock, they go to bed.

MOTHER: There's something the matter with that, though. We already have a bedtime. The problem is that they still go past their bedtime because they fall asleep.

MIKE: Because it's vacation.

MOTHER: It wasn't vacation last week, and bedtime is eight-thirty on school nights, and at eight-thirty you were asleep on the family room floor.

FATHER: I don't want to be put in a position where I have to be a . . .

ED: Traffic cop.

FATHER: Yeah, to go around saying, "Bedtime, bedtime."

MOTHER: That's what would happen if we accepted number two?

FATHER: I don't want to accept it.

MIKE: All right, then number one is more work. Wake up a person once.

FATHER: I don't want to do that. That's what I said.

MOTHER: How about you?

MIKE: I like it.

FATHER: But I don't want to do it.

MOTHER: What would be wrong if we accepted one of their solutions? How do you feel about it?

FATHER: I told you.

MIKE: That would be great.

ED: Our solution would work better, because we like it.

FATHER: I told you, I don't want to be the judge and ruler. I don't want to go around saying, "Bedtime, bedtime."

MIKE: You don't have to.

FATHER: You put me in a position of taking care of your responsibilities.

MIKE: How about waking up a person once?

MOTHER: We could change that a little bit.

FATHER: How?

MOTHER: Instead of at their bedtime . . .

FATHER: The problem is that the boys fall asleep on the floor . . .

MOTHER: And they don't like . . .

FATHER: And they don't like being left because they have to get up and go to bed by themselves when they wake up.

MIKE: And it hurts, and it's cold.

FATHER: Well, that's the natural consequence of that situation.

MOTHER: I agree.

FATHER: And I'm not going to interfere with it. I'm not going to say, "Time to go to bed, Ed." So I think we have to forget about solving this problem this week and just let it go.

At the following week's meeting of the Family Council, the problem of bedtime and the boys falling asleep on the floor was the first one to come up:

ED: Last night everybody left me on the couch. I don't like it.

FATHER: Let's start where we left off last week. We had three or four problems that we couldn't solve. The first one was that the boys don't like being left out. Now if Mike will read the list, there were four suggestions.

MIKE: "Mom and dad wake us up once; bedtime should be established; no blankets or pillows allowed; whoever falls asleep in family room must get self to bed with no help from anyone else." How did the fourth one get on there?

MOTHER: That was dad's suggestion.

FATHER: Now can we discuss the suggestions one at a time and see which one we would like to try?

MIKE: No.

MOTHER: Or would you like to add some others, since we could come to no agreement on any of these? First of all, we could scratch the second one because we're going back to schooltime hours, and that's not a problem.

MIKE: Then our problem is solved. Eight-thirty is bedtime. That's it. So we don't have to talk about it any more.

FATHER: But I'm not . . .

MIKE: But I'm going to go to bed at eight-thirty from now on.

FATHER: But dad still will not tell you what time to go to bed.

MIKE: I know.

FATHER: You know it's eight-thirty.

MIKE: Yeah.

FATHER: Ed, do you know when it's eight-thirty?

ED: When one hand is on the eight and the other is on the six.

FATHER: And do you know what to do when it's eight-thirty?

ED: Go to bed.

MIKE: All right. Next problem.

FATHER: Are we all in agreement that this is the way it's going to be?

ED: But on Saturdays and Sundays . . .

FATHER: Fridays and Saturdays you can stay up. Nobody tells you when to go to bed.

MOTHER: If you fall asleep on the floor, you're still responsible for getting yourself to bed.

ED: Right.

MOTHER: It's not our job to see to it that you are waked up to go to bed. You're on your own.

MIKE: Right.

MOTHER: That's it. Then our problem is solved.

What had been a continuing source of disagreement in the family, what couldn't be solved in one meeting, worked out well when it was delayed for a week. Nothing was lost except the possibility for argument. Instead of keeping the subject at the boiling point, the fire had been turned off by a week's postponement. The issue was settled finally in reasonable discussion.

8

Coping with Conflict

The procedure we propose is not to avoid conflicts, but to solve them. There will always be conflicts, for each human being first sees problems only from his own perspective. In an autocratic society, the one who had the most strength made the decision, and the others had to accept it.

In the family, the father was the one who told the others what to do. If they resisted, punishment was swift and severe. It was necessary for the "superior" person to show his "inferiors" that he was indeed boss—he had to beat the others down.

However, the democratic revolution all over the world has meant a change in human relationships. The child who is punished decides, "If you have the right to punish me, I can punish you," and then proceeds to do so. Typically, he watches and listens until he finds out just what it is that his parents can't stand, and then he does it. This warfare is at the bottom of most family conflicts.

Parents, seeing children as their enemies, keep them down, keep them dependent, keep them largely helpless. Children, seeing parents as their enemies, use a lot of energy and thought to outwit them. Both generations deprive themselves of the chance to live together in harmony, and to use that energy for ideas and activities that will make their lives together more fun.

As long as there are conflicts, everybody can learn to solve them—not avoid them, not fight over them, but find agreement. Agreement is reached when everybody feels he has gained something from the decision. Compromise is a situation in which everybody, giving up something, feels that he has lost.

There are four actions necessary to solve conflicts democratically. They are:
1. *Create mutual respect*
2. *Pinpoint the issue*
3. *Seek areas of agreement*
4. *Share responsibilities*

Create Mutual Respect

In the family—as well as in any other group, whether it is in the classroom, the business office, the factory, or the field—each of the persons in the group must respect the others as worthy human beings. There can be no superior and inferior. There are different persons with different roles in the group, but each is entitled to contribute, and to have his contribution treated with respect.

Nothing can be accomplished by one person's domination except to convince all the others that they have no chance. One person may be older, one better educated, one more experienced; but all have the right to be heard.

In the Family Council, rotation of the offices of chairman and secretary is a concrete method of demonstrating the equal worth of all family members. Listening to each person is one of the ways to create mutual respect; accepting the ideas and contributions of each member is another. Gradually, in the effort to reach democratic living, children will blossom in the sunshine of respect, and will in turn give respect to their parents, sisters, and brothers.

Pinpoint the Issue

In any conflict, it is necessary to discover and pinpoint the issue. The real issue is never what people are arguing about. The issue is the disturbed human relationship.

When children resist requests that parents believe to be reasonable, it is not the requests themselves that the child resists, but the domination.

When siblings fight over something that everybody knows they don't really care about, what they're really fighting for is mother's attention. They're fighting to see who is the favorite, or who is more powerful, or who can arouse the biggest excitement.

In the Family Council, every person decides what to do, without even knowing it. Unless agreement really represents everyone's contribution, it is no agreement. Children will not be bound by decisions in which they feel they have had no part. They will find ways to avoid complying.

The underlying issue will usually be seen as one of the following:

1. *A threat to personal status—"Why should I give in?"*
2. *A question of prestige—"What will they think?"*
3. *A matter of superiority—"If I'm not on top, I'll be on the bottom."*
4. *The right to decide—"Why should I let him decide for me?"*
5. *The right to control—"If I don't boss them, they won't do it right."*
6. *The right of judgment—"Whose way is the best way?"*
7. *The idea of retaliation—"He won the last one."*
8. *The wish for revenge—"I'll get even this time."*

When people are fighting, there is great cooperation. They are cooperating by continuing to fight with one another, by keeping the conflict going so that it won't get stopped at a loss to any participant. Only when each individual can stop fighting long enough to decide what he or she is willing to do by himself, without demanding from anybody else, can effective agreement be reached.

Seek Areas of Agreement

Having identified the issue, every possible way to agree must be explored. Under the title "brainstorming," business has invented the group meeting in which everybody bounces ideas off everybody else. In the Family Council, the democratic way to seek agreement is to encourage each member to express an idea, no matter how farfetched it may seem. From the combination of the work of several minds comes the way out of the conflict.

In this effort, the recorder is more necessary then the negotiator. If every possibility is written down, no ideas are lost; and out of the minds of all members will come the agreement to satisfy everybody.

The family is the laboratory in which we can test out the possibility of creating a new emotional climate for all mankind. What we can develop is beyond our present imagination. In the Family Council, children as well as parents learn how to cope with conflict and how to solve conflict in a democratic manner.

Typically, each of us involved in a conflict knows only what the other person is doing wrong, and each one wants to tell the other one what he should do to straighten out. But the only person anyone can change is himself—when I change, my opponent has to change. Only when I begin to think about what I can do to change can I affect the people around me.

There's no predicament so bad that there is no alternative—a better way or a worse way. Together we must seek those alternatives in order to find the better way.

When parents feel that the situation is so bad it can't possibly get any worse, they must realize that life is an ongoing process, and nothing can stop its movement.

The worst way out of a predicament is through one person's domination—the best way will be found through joint effort.

Share Responsibilities

Like the search for agreement, the responsibility for the agreement reached must be shared. Leadership must be democratic, not autocratic.

The Family Council provides the framework in which the whole family learns to share the work of the family life. In the household as well as in the classroom, it's no good if one person does all the work. It is not the mother, not both parents, not the teacher, not just adults who are the workers; all who are part of the process must share in the responsibilities.

This means that the children as well as the adults have the freedom to try out new ideas, new methods, new areas of learning. Children are striving and creating all the time—the task of the adults, whether they are parents or teachers, is to release them from the necessity to rebel and instead encourage them to participate.

9

Sharing Responsibilities

In previous generations, families lived according to the traditions handed down by their parents. Each family, dependent on its own labor for its food, shelter, and clothing, had more work than two adults could handle. Families depended on every child to do his share of the work as soon as he was able. There was men's work and women's work, and then there were chores for children.

In today's world, where very little of the actual production of necessities is done in the home, the traditional jobs have disappeared. Parents usually think of their children's help when it's time to take out the garbage or walk the dog.

At the same time, the technological era has given us possessions and machinery that our forefathers never dreamed of, and all these things require care. In the days when children shared a bed and owned only a few clothes, mothers didn't need to holler "Clean up your room!" There wasn't much to clean up. Nor were there many toys to strew around the living quarters, and certainly no television to hypnotize them. Recreation was something the children made for themselves with very little equipment. It was not purchased, arranged, and programmed by parents.

We cannot turn the clock back, and we wouldn't know how to act if we did. But we can't deny that the ways in which we live in the last third of the twentieth century require far different arrangements.

One of the ways in which children can experience participation in the work of the family is to share in the responsibilities. This doesn't mean that mother or father, or both parents together, decide who should take out the garbage, and who should do the dishes. Rather, the family together should figure out what's involved, and then together sort out the tasks according to ability and interest.

When parents assign jobs to children, children feel resentful. Especially if they have not previously been required to do anything but exist and enjoy, they will feel imposed upon. However, when children can learn all that goes into the family function, they will see how their own contribution is important and valued. Every family differs in its living arrangements, but all arrangements need work. It is not possible to rank the responsibilities according to importance, and it is not necessary. Every family member can have a job he can perform without help. Even the youngest can enjoy the dignity of doing something for which the whole family depends on him.

So that readers can discover what needs to be done in their own households, the following outline has been compiled from talks with many families:

Family Responsibilities

Outside

Sweep	Porch
	Sidewalk
	Patio
Clear	Snow
Bring in	Newspaper
Put out	Garbage

Inside

Dust	Furniture
	Bookshelves
	Piano
	Hi-fi; TV
Vacuum	Carpets
	Rugs
	Floors
Empty	Ashtrays
	Wastebaskets
	Garage
Mop	Floors
Scrub	Sinks
	Bathtubs
	Toilets
Wipe	Light switches

Kitchen

Shop and put away	
Prepare and cook meals	
Table	Set
	Clear
	Wipe

Dishes and utensils	Scrape
	Rinse
	Wash
	Dry
Dishwasher	Load
	Empty
Stove	Clean
Refrigerator	Wash

Laundry

Collection
   Linens

Strip beds
Put on clean sheets
Remove towels from bathroom
Replace with clean towels

   Clothing

Pick up and put in laundry
Empty pockets
Sort according to color

Wash
Dry
Iron
Fold
Hang
Sort
Deliver to user

Sewing

Mend
Darn
Replace buttons
New clothes
Household items

Pets

Feed

Buy
Prepare
Serve
Clean
Give fresh water

Perform sanitary services

Take outdoors: A.M.; P.M.
Clean litter box or cage

Exercise
Bathe and brush

Care for others

Transportation   Doctor
                                            Dentist
                                            School
                                            Special lessons
                                            Sports
                                            Activities
Siblings   Baby-sitting
  Infant   Diapers
                                            Bottle
                                            Attend
  Toddler   Watch
                                            Toilet
                                            Read to
                                            Clothe

Other relatives
  Aged or infirm   Accompany
                                            Visit
                                            Read to
                                            Play games with
                                            Walk with
                                            Assist

Toys

Keep in order
Put away
Clean
Repair
Store in appropriate place

Financial and clerical

Earn income
Provide sustenance
Balance budget
Pay bills
Keep records

Maintenance

Routine   Cut the grass

Specific

> Rake grass clippings
> Rake leaves
> Pull the weeds
> Trim trees and hedges
> Sweep sidewalks
> Shovel snow
> Replace furnace filters
> Change light bulbs
> Make minor repairs
> Wash windows
> Paint
> Wallpaper

Automobile

Wash	Vacuum inside
Get gas and oil	

Errands

Clothes to cleaner or laundry
Shoes to be repaired
Drugstore
Library
Shopping other than food
Things to be fixed
Things to be cleaned

The above list can serve as a starting point. The jobs are not equal, or of equal value to the family, but each person can find one to perform. More can be added, and some can be subtracted.

Some jobs may be divided further. For instance, in many families it is not one person's sole responsibility to earn the family income. Many mothers earn part of it; many young adults earn their share. Their contributions are not equal, but all are to be respected. Similarly, those tasks that do not contribute tangible results are to be respected.

In the Fallon family, there are five children: Chuck, almost 11; Joan and Jane, 9-year-old twins; Dale, 8; and Kevin, 4½. Chuck had chosen not to attend the meeting from which the following is taken, so there were six participants, and they began by going over their family's job list:

FATHER: What is today's date, secretary?
DALE: April 18.
FATHER: Would you please restate what we all agreed to just now?
DALE: We all voted to tape the family meeting.

FATHER: All right. Does anybody have a subject to bring up at this meeting?

JOAN: Guess the jobs.

DALE: OK. Is there anyone who wants to sign up for table?

JANE: I will.

DALE: OK. Rinse?

JOAN: I will.

DALE: Load?

JANE: I will.

DALE: Pots and pans—I will. Sweep and garbage—Chuck.

MOTHER: Chuck?

DALE: Kevin?

MOTHER: What's left? Oh, wiping the refrigerator and stove and dishwasher. Can you do that, Kevin? Are you big enough to do that? Do you know how to do it? Who'd like to offer to show Kevin how to do that job?

In her exuberance over encouraging a young child to do an important job, mother is demeaning him. She shows a lack of respect for Kevin by questioning his ability. It is far better to let him decide whether this is a job he can tackle, knowing that if it proves to be beyond his ability he can say so at the next meeting. His response to mother shows that he is eager to take it on.

KEVIN: I already know how.

MOTHER: That's great. Do you need a helper?

KEVIN: No.

MOTHER: OK. Real good.

DALE: Daddy?

FATHER: Is that all the jobs?

DALE: Yes.

FATHER: Would you please read off the jobs and the names?

DALE: Yes. "Table, Jane. Rinse, Joan. Load, Jane. Pots and pans, Dale. Sweep and garbage, Chuck."

FATHER: I don't think we have all the jobs down.

DALE: "Refrigerator, stove: Kevin."

MOTHER: Who's load?

DALE: Jane.

JANE: Somebody should help Kevin with the hot stuff.

KEVIN: No, I'll do it myself. I can't do inside the stove.

DALE: I think outside will be all right. Kevin, do you have anything to say?

MOTHER: I think Kevin has done very well on his jobs. That was his first time on the last job, and I think he really did a good job of it; that's a big job, to load the dishwasher. I don't know anybody else four years old that does it. I think with a chair—if he just stood on a chair—I think he could reach the refrigerator. Think you could, Kevin?

KEVIN: With a chair, yes.
DALE: I think that's good, for a four-year-old. I think that's good.
JANE: Kevin has had to lean over to get stuff, though.
MOTHER: Why don't we let him try?
KEVIN: To lean over backwards?
DALE: No, to do the wiping job. You'll be able to.

The Fallons have learned the principles of sharing responsibility, and encourage the youngest to take on a job that he feels he can do. There is certainly some question in the mind of the mother, who still speaks protectively, but the four-year-old grows under the confidence placed in him.

In the Gordon family, there are only two children, Gail, age 8, who is chairman of this meeting, and David, age 6. They too have a job list, but they treat the jobs as specific entities, and do not yet have the idea of sharing genuine responsibilities.

The Gordons have a job list which is limited to a very few of the regular routines in the household. Some of the jobs are specifically the responsibility of the parents: the laundry, which mother found more expedient to do herself; and walking the dog, which is big and too difficult for the children to control.

The jobs they share are:

> Taking out the garbage
> Doing the laundry
> Setting the table
> Stacking the dishwasher
> Bringing in newspaper
> Bringing down dad's slippers
> Putting away groceries
> Watering plants

The excerpt which follows demonstrates how they handle their job list in their meeting:

FATHER: Let's start. Who's chairman?
MOTHER: Gail.
FATHER: OK, Gail. Let's go.

In these three comments, these parents already show their domination, and their lack of respect for the children. Father decides that it's time to start; although Gail is right there, mother answers that Gail is the chairman. Thus, as the meeting begins, both parents show their lack of respect for their children, and their subconscious intention to stay in control.

GAIL: Who wants garbage?
DAVID: Daddy. You do a good job of it.

FATHER: Do I do a good job? I did a fantastic job.
MOTHER: I'll take garbage.
GAIL: Who wants laundry?
MOTHER: I think we should . . .
DAVID: I want laundry.
MOTHER: Wait a minute. I have something to say about laundry. I don't think that's a good job for the job list. Because I do it at weird times and things.

It is apparent that mother thinks of the job list as something superficial—minor tasks that can be parceled out. She has not yet realized that she belittles the children's responsibilities when she speaks in this way.

GAIL: You know, she does it when no one's around.
MOTHER: The laundry job never gets done, so I think we should scrap it. I don't like having jobs like that on the list.

Mother has wasted the opportunity for the entire family to talk over the reason why the "laundry job never gets done." She, as well as the others, could have learned something from listening to one another as they talked about the nature of the job.

GAIL: You've got to make a motion.
MOTHER: I make a motion that we eliminate laundry from the job list for now.
GAIL: How many are in favor? OK, setting the table.
FATHER: Who had it last week?
GAIL: I had it the week before.
FATHER: Who had it last week?
GAIL: The week before that mommy had it.
FATHER: Setting the table. That's kind of hard, 'cause when I come home from work . . .
MOTHER: That's not a good daddy job.
GAIL: I know, but it's a good mommy job. And I had it the week before.
DAVID: And I had it the week before that.
MOTHER: All right. I'll have it next week.

In treating the question of jobs in this way, with certain ones not to be done by daddy, and others not to be done by the children, the family loses sight of the concept of sharing responsibilities. What they have done is to create an artificial list of tasks they're willing to talk about, and so they pretend to deal with vital issues.

An illustration of their misconception recurs when they discuss the "groceries" job:

GAIL: What about groceries?
MOTHER: I don't want groceries.

DAVID: Daddy? Gail, it's up to you.
GAIL: No, it isn't. I've got two jobs. Mommy's got two jobs.
DAVID: Well, I don't want groceries again.
FATHER: You can have two jobs. Don't you think you can start taking a couple?
MOTHER: OK, you want to set the table?
DAVID: And you'll take the groceries?
MOTHER: Yes.
DAVID: No, I'd rather have groceries.
MOTHER: All right. I have something to say about groceries. I feel that whoever is on groceries is capable of putting them all away.
GAIL: That's not what we said when we first started. It was for help—just for help.
DAVID: Then I'm not going to take groceries.
GAIL: That's what jobs are for—helping, not for doing them all by yourself.

Here Gail speaks her incorrect idea. She has not learned the principle of sharing responsibility, but still sees herself as a junior member of the family who is only capable of helping the grown-ups. If this were all that children could do, mother would always have all the responsibility, and only hope the children would help when she especially asks them.

The effect of this on mother is shown in her response. She sounds like the typical martyr who can't depend on anyone else, but has to do it herself:

MOTHER: Wait a minute. David, let's decide what this job of groceries is first, and then we'll decide who's willing to take it. There seems to be some misunderstanding. Last week David was on groceries. I brought the groceries into the kitchen and put away some of them. When I came down to make dinner the rest of them were all over, so I did put them away. But I believe that everybody in this house is capable of putting away groceries.
GAIL: No, it wasn't made as a rule that we were to do it all alone.
DAVID: That's why I waited for you.
MOTHER: Then I would like to change it. Do you remember how that rule was? We need a whole book of rules.

The only reason mother feels that they need a whole book of rules is that they haven't understood the basic principles of sharing responsibilities. What they need is not a book of rules, but rather a rethinking of how they act toward one another. Father sounds as though he wants mother to continue to be the one who does everything; mother wants help, but if she doesn't get it, she'll do it herself and complain, as mothers have been doing for years.

Each of these family members is still concerned about getting his own rights and not letting others get away with anything. By thinking in terms of who helps whom, they have lost sight of the work that needs to be done for the comfort of all.

Continuing the discussion about rules, they say:

FATHER: It was to be only a help.

MOTHER: All right. Now I would like to change the rule. I would like to make it that whoever has the groceries job that week is responsible for putting them all away.

GAIL: You have to make a motion first.

FATHER: Let's talk about it. If anybody has any feelings about it . . .

DAVID: I don't think we should change the rule.

FATHER: Well, I think that everybody is big enough now—it's not that big a job.

The issue is not whether the children are big enough. It is that they have not been allowed to feel equal. There is a spirit of "parents know best" throughout the comments, and the natural result is that the children resist. No matter what they say in this meeting, they know that if they fail to do their jobs, mother will take over.

Father does not realize that the crucial point is that only mother goes out to shop for groceries, and brings them into the house. For anyone else to put them away requires that someone be present and available to do so when she returns.

FATHER: When it's mommy's turn to do it, then she has to do it all by herself.

DAVID: And when it's your turn to do it, you have to do it all alone.

GAIL: I can really see daddy doing it.

Gail already understands that father considers certain jobs beneath his dignity, fit only for women and children.

DAVID: Why couldn't you do it, daddy?

FATHER: Do you want the groceries all left out until I come home from work?

DAVID: Yes.

FATHER: That means mother wouldn't be able to use them to make dinner.

DAVID: You mean, we wouldn't be able to eat until you put the groceries away?

FATHER: Right. Or suppose I was out of town that day, and didn't come home that night?

DAVID: Then we wouldn't be able to eat at all.

FATHER: That's right. OK—let's decide whether or not the groceries really should be . . . whether the person that has the job should do the whole job of putting them away.

MOTHER: Because it could also work that, if I had them, I could ask the children to help.

GAIL: I don't care.

MOTHER: I make a motion that groceries be one person's responsibility to do the whole job.

GAIL: How many are in favor? How many opposed?

MOTHER: Two to two, so it stays the way it is.

The subject has come to a standstill, and will come up again, unless the adults realize that they are attempting the impossible. They are acting as if they were the traditional autocrats, while trying to talk as though they lead democratically.

The autocratic attitude can best be seen by examining the lines father speaks in the beginning of the foregoing scenario, when it is father who says "Let's start." When he is informed who the chairman is, he says "Let's go" as though he has to give the starter's signal before anything can happen.

When father speaks of the garbage, he says "I did a fantastic job" which may sound like a joke, but in his use of exaggeration he indicates his contempt for this menial job.

The next task is setting the table, and although Gail is chairman, father asks the questions. It is he who says, "Who had it last week?" as though his daughter were incapable of carrying on. And so it goes on, with the children resisting and the parents proposing. There is also the continuing undercurrent of father's importance. The result is a deadlock.

No harm has been done by avoiding a decision, however. Mother will continue to be the person who goes to get the groceries, who brings them in, and probably who puts them away. Other alternatives might have arisen; for instance, could mother agree to put away all perishables, and leave the staples for another family member? In what other ways might this be handled so that it becomes a part of the total family's responsibility?

It would be necessary for the job list to include more of the real work. As it is, it covers so few tasks, and such small ones at that, that it is difficult for anyone to take it very seriously.

If all the work the family requires were to be taken into consideration, father would have his fair share. His being away from home is required by his responsibility of earning the family income. There are other responsibilities in the household he could assume in his turn—those that he could perform on the days or evenings when he is at home. Each job a family member undertakes must be his own responsibility.

We do not mean to indicate that one family member must not ask another for help, but rather that each person voluntarily chooses a task within his ability. The risk in having a child report to a parent for instruction is that the child will see this as being bossed, and will resent it.

The object of having each person have specific tasks is that it helps the family to move toward the time when most requests and commands are eliminated. When each person knows where the responsibilities lie, natural consequences help to enforce performance and much of the daily conflict is avoided.

10

Special Tasks

In every household, there are special jobs that come up only once in a great while. The customary pattern is for the parents to become concerned about the appearance of something around the house: the garden is overgrown, the rug is dirty, the garage is messy. Usually the children have different standards of appearance than the parents, and don't care how things look.

The old pattern was for parents to beg, cajole, bribe, or command that their children help. In families that are trying to be democratic, it's difficult to find a different way to get the work done, but the Family Council provides the setting. Often, even offering to pay for labor doesn't appeal to the children; but when they can see the work as a contribution to the general family welfare, they are more likely to be willing. And, of course, willing work is the most productive.

Here's how the Stone family handled an onerous job:

FATHER: Could I bring up some new business?
BRAD: It's out of order, but we'll overlook it.
FATHER: We've just about got the weeding licked, and I wondered if we could set up some sort of an agreement on working together the rest of the week to finish it off. What do you think about weeding for a half hour every day at a certain time—everybody doing it—except me? I'll be at work.

Father has assumed that everybody else wants the weeding done as much as he does, which is probably incorrect. Then he belittles the job by saying, "I'll be at work," which means, "You three can do it; I have more important things to do." The resulting evasion is easy to predict. There's no way the other members of his family will be enthusiastic about doing a job he looks down on.

63

MOTHER: I've got another idea. How about zooming for two hours tonight, and get it done?

Mother would like to have father's participation, and would like to get the job finished soon. But father doesn't hear her.

FATHER: Is anybody interested in weeding the rest of next week? Half hour every day?
BRAD: How about saying, "Is anybody interested in weeding?" I'm not interested in weeding a half hour every day, because I can't guarantee I'll be able to do it every day. When you start doing daily things like that it gets overbearing.

Brad, age 20, has made his point when he implies that no one is interested in weeding. If that could come out in the open, something might be accomplished in mutual understanding. But the parents go on trying to reach a standard for the job they want done.

MOTHER: What about fifteen minutes? Of course anybody can work longer, but what about a minimum of fifteen minutes instead of half an hour?
SKIP: Okay.
FATHER: What time do you want to do it?
BRAD: Let's make it whenever we want to.
SKIP: How about at your convenience? Is that agreeable?
FATHER: How will anybody know that everybody's done it?

Father still isn't willing to trust the others to do what he wants done. They may agree now but if they don't feel that there was democratic participation, each one will do whatever he wants.

BRAD: Let's go on the honor system.
FATHER: Well, everybody's here at six o'clock in the morning. Why don't we do it at six o'clock?
MOTHER: Why don't we each be on our honor to do fifteen minutes of weeding, more than that if we can spare the time, and then we'll discuss it next time and see if everybody's done it.
FATHER: How about when the fellow does his weeding, he comes in and announces to everybody that he's done his weeding?
BRAD: It sounds kind of like . . . there's something wrong with it.

Brad can't express exactly what he feels, but he knows he's being pushed against his will in a roundabout way. If father were to issue an order, Brad would promptly resist; and they might fight. This way, they're not fighting, but they're not moving toward agreement either. Father says he's the boss, he wants it done; and Brad feels he's not going to be bossed, no matter how it's presented.

FATHER: My point is that we've almost got it whipped now.

BRAD: Why does anybody have to announce to everybody that he's done the weeding? Doesn't anybody trust anybody?

FATHER: Well, all I'm going on is past experience when we say we're going to do things and somehow they don't get done.

BRAD: If nobody trusts anybody, how are you going to believe the guy when he comes in and says he's done the weeding. What's the difference?

MOTHER: Let's just bring it up next time. Everybody do fifteen minutes a day, and then we'll bring it up and see if everybody did it. And if everybody did it, no problem; and if everybody didn't, then we'll work out why it didn't get done.

FATHER: OK.

BRAD: OK, I'm in agreement with that. Put it in the minutes, Skip.

SKIP: OK.

Mother diffused the issue by suggesting that the subject come up again next week. By that time, all would have had a chance to reflect, and there would be evidence on which to base a new discussion.

The critical point is that father wants the weeding to be finished. The children probably don't care about the weeds at all. Father expects everyone's help, with the least expenditure of his own effort. Adult standards of appearance are usually influenced by "what the neighbors will think." Their children may not care at all about the condition of the grounds, or may in fact prefer surroundings in which they can feel free to romp, rather than a well-groomed yard in which they must be careful. Nevertheless, an atmosphere of mutual respect will help the children to recognize their responsibility to do unattractive chores, just as parents do things for their children that are inconvenient or burdensome.

Some special tasks involve future fun for the family, but first the actual work must be shared. The Curtis family is looking forward to the summer season when they will all enjoy their backyard pool, which is not a permanent installation.

FATHER: I want to bring up the swimming pool. I started to put it up today, and we need to get together and make up some rules and regulations, so if anybody has anything to . . .

ED: Let's try to get that up today, and try filling it up with water. It will take all night to fill it up with water, so maybe tomorrow we'll be able to go in it.

MOTHER: What are the processes we have to go through to get the pool set up?

MIKE: We have to get a Roto-Tiller.

FATHER: We have to dig it out and set it up level and . . .

ED: Well, with some real manpower we wouldn't need a Roto-Tiller. We could get it done.

MOTHER: How deep does it have to be dug?

FATHER: About two feet.

ED: We have the manpower to do that easily in about three hours. And it wouldn't hurt.

MIKE: With the three of us doing it, we could do it maybe in less than three hours.

FATHER: We can get started as soon as we finish the meeting.

The Harris family has three sons: Ken, 11; Larry, 10; and Jeff, 7. Here's how it was when father brought up the subject of dirty clothes:

FATHER: There's a stack of clothes downstairs, Larry. They are too muddy to be washed. Does anybody have any ideas what we ought to do about them?

LARRY: How about . . .

JEFF: No.

FATHER: He didn't call on you. He's the chairman.

Note that father wasn't called on, either. In the act of telling his son that he is not the chairman, father is butting in, just as much as Larry is. Father has not relinquished his role as ruler.

LARRY: He won't call on me, because he's got a suggestion.

FATHER: Well, let's hear his. He's the chairman.

JEFF: Well, I think Larry and I should clean the clothes that are ours. He's got many of his down there. And some of them are mine, so I should clean those.

KEN: They can't be put into the . . .

MOTHER: They can't be put into the washing machine until the mud is dried and taken off them.

JEFF: I know. But they're already dry.

KEN: I think you ought to put them in the person's room. Let them stay there until . . .

LARRY: Forget it.

FATHER: Why would you want to get the room all dirty?

KEN: It's their clothes.

JEFF: Ken, it's our room.

KEN: Too bad, isn't it?

LARRY: How would you like us to put some dirty clothes in your room?

KEN: I wouldn't mind if they were mine.

FATHER: I don't think this is a solution.

KEN: What are you going to do? Isn't it their responsibility?

MOTHER: All right, that was Ken's suggestion. Does somebody have a better solution?

LARRY: Yeah. Have 'em go down and clean it up.

KEN: Larry, if a person doesn't do it by force, what makes you think he's gonna do it voluntarily?

MOTHER: Well, we hope that he will.

LARRY: If he doesn't, then you could just give it to the rummage sale.

MOTHER: All right, I kind of like Ken's idea. They look terrible in our backyard, all piled up on that little patio table. There are four pairs of slacks, and at least one shirt—I don't even know whose they all are.

LARRY: I still don't want the dirty clothes in my room, because then they would just end up on Jeff's bed, and then he just throws them on the floor.

MOTHER: I can't blame you. What could we do about it, then? What can be done about it? They've been out there at least a week.

LARRY: Jeff should go down there and clean them up.

JEFF: And you too.

LARRY: If he doesn't clean them up, he won't have them to wear.

FATHER: Well, what are we going to do about it, and how soon?

MOTHER: Larry just said—it's up to the individual to take care of his clothes. And it's not up to dad to replace clothes that aren't taken care of.

The question of the muddy clothes having been settled, later in the same meeting the Harris family met another problem about the laundry:

MOTHER: I have better than a week's washing downstairs that was thrown down all at one time, but I really don't feel much like doing it, because I was all caught up with my washing when that was thrown down, all in a bunch.

LARRY: Don't do it.

KEN: I don't think that's fair to Larry or Jeff or me or whoever the person was who put it there.

LARRY: But it was from Jeff's bed.

KEN: I don't care whose it is. It pertains to all of us. You get the wash at night.

JEFF: Last week it was your stuff that I threw down.

MOTHER: He's right, Larry. Quite a bit . . .

KEN: Collect it in your own bed.

MOTHER: Really, I feel like a slave when I have to do . . . when I'm all caught up in my washing and I have to start a whole week's wash and do it in one day. Because that's when you kids decide to throw it down.

KEN: I think you ought to make the people who are throwing it down do it, because I know that when I throw down the clothes I do it every day, not all at once in a bunch.

Ken is expressing his superiority as the eldest, speaking as if mother has the power over the others, and he won't be affected because he does his job properly. Mother is losing sight of the fact that the way to stop feeling like a slave is to stop acting like one. She pleads:

MOTHER: I need some help, boys. Do I have to do it all before you kids run out of clothes? Or what?

FATHER: How about having the guys who threw it down end up putting it in the washing machine?

The simplest way, the natural consequence of what the boys have done, would be for mother to stay away from the washing machine until the next time she wants to do the total family laundry. But father is anxious to get the decision made, preferably according to his ideas.

Mother worries that her sons may not have clean clothes to wear, and would not look presentable, which she would then perceive as her fault. Father at least realizes that with automatic equipment, the burden need not be on mother, but each family member can wash his own clothes.

Mother doesn't want to let it go at that, and pursues:

MOTHER: Putting the clothes in and putting soap in the washing machine is nothing. How about the folding, or if there's anything that has to be ironed . . .
FATHER: They'll be responsible for the whole thing.
MOTHER: Then I'll wash them.
FATHER: Is that agreeable?
MOTHER: And bring them up just the way they are, and you guys take care of the rest? How about that?

Mother wants to have it her way, so that she can continue to feel responsible, but her sons don't want her to feel like a slave:

JEFF: Mommy, the stuff that was Larry's, you know what he could do? He could wash his own and I could wash my own. That would be saving time.
FATHER: It was suggested that when mom washes and dries them, Jeff, you and Larry will sit down and fold them and put them away.
MOTHER: If you want to wash 'em and dry 'em, that's it, as long as they tell me when they're going to use the machines.
FATHER: Well, what do you think?
LARRY: Let's do it. We'll do it.
KEN: Well, all right, forget it—that's enough.
MOTHER: What's your decision, boys? What are you going to do?

Mother isn't listening to what they have proposed to do, but wants a final decision that will allow her to suffer for their neglect. She falls back with a threat:

LARRY: We'll fold them.
MOTHER: I'll tell you something. If it happens again, I'll wash them at my convenience, not when you boys run out of clothes. Because I don't think you're thinking about me when you do it, do you?

JEFF: No.

FATHER: Come on, Jeff.

MOTHER: So what was the agreement?

LARRY: That Jeff and I would . . .

MOTHER: That this time . . .

LARRY: That Jeff and I would, after you wash them, put them in the dryer and stuff like that.

MOTHER: What if it happens again?

LARRY: We're going to have to do it ourselves.

JEFF: Is everybody through with that one?

LARRY: Yes.

This matter won't be settled until mother stops feeling sorry for her sons, and lets them experience the results of their own negligence. As long as they hold family meetings regularly, anyone who is dissatisfied with the way things have been going in the home can bring up his dissatisfaction and have it heard. The process of arriving at an agreement is difficult, and takes time, but on the way everyone's attitudes can be expressed and considered.

The Jensen family were holding their meeting before the planned birthday party for the oldest daughter, Ruth:

MOTHER: I have one more thing to say. We've got company coming for Ruthie's birthday dinner today, and this means a whole lot of potatoes to peel, and a big salad to make, and the table to set with eight extra places. Does anybody want to help with that?

FRED: I'll work like a dog until two, but I want to watch the game at two o'clock.

RHODA: You said I could do the salad.

MOTHER: OK, Fred, what do you want to do?

FRED: I'll do whatever you want that needs to be done.

FATHER: I cleaned up the kitchen and put all the breakfast dishes away.

RHODA: Let's adjourn, so we can go into the kitchen and get started.

This mother doesn't sound as though she feels responsible for the whole dinner, but rather that the children are capable of sharing in the work as well as sharing in the festivities. Her control of the kitchen is not at stake. By being willing to let others take on part of the work, and letting them choose what they will do, the party becomes the family's, rather than something mother does for them.

The Jensens have caught on to the idea of productive work by willing workers.

11

Common Mistakes

The Parkers are trying hard to be democratic, to treat one another as equals, but it's a very difficult task. Like most parents, they have not been aware of their underlying attitudes, which keep getting in the way of their words. Any statement any member of the family makes reveals his attitude toward his relationship with others. When parents begin to realize what underlies their spoken words, they can begin to catch themselves and make progress toward democracy.

Both Allen and Mabel Parker are sincere and well-intentioned as they participate in the Family Council. They are quite autocratic, however, and the meeting becomes an argument rather than an open, friendly discussion.

Their children are Meg, 9; Glenn, 7; and Jim, 2. Jim does not participate in the meeting which follows:

MEG: I'd like to talk about allowances. I think we should raise allowances now that I'm nine.
FATHER: Raise them to what?

This is the first indication of the underlying power conflict in the family. Father's response doesn't mean he wants to know what the allowances should be raised to—he's already suspicious of raising them at all, and nothing good can come of this. His words indicate his hostile attitude. He has not yet learned to listen to his daughter with respect.

Glenn is worried that he'll be left out, and his anxiety is indicated as he responds.

GLENN: So I'm seven.
MOTHER: I don't know what to raise them to . . .

71

Mother's comment indicates a genuine concern over the amount of the allowances. But father is not genuinely concerned. He challenges:

FATHER: How about, how about . . .
GLENN: A dollar?
FATHER: How about 16¢ and 26¢?
GLENN: A dollar.
FATHER: No, a dollar is too much.

Father immediately makes an issue over what is right, instead of helping to create an atmosphere of thinking the problem through together. A more democratic response would have been:

FATHER: Meg wants a bigger allowance. Let's have a free discussion about whether she should get more, and how much. And Glenn too. Let's all talk it over.

As soon as father says, "How about 16¢ and 26¢?" he's in the midst of a power conflict. He's not willing to discuss the merits of the situation; he's already questioning his daughter's rights, and is provoking a fight. Mother is not interested in a fight, but father is. He is utterly unaware of his own hostility, as both parents are unaware of how they are fighting with each other.

It is quite clear that father is the boss. He is not prepared to listen to anyone. He is an excellent example of the average parent who tries to participate in a Family Council. He's willing, but hasn't the slightest idea of how to go about it—how to talk and how to listen.

MOTHER: You mean you want more than a quarter a week?
MEG: Well, maybe a quarter, but to spend more on things.
MOTHER: You want to be able to spend more than a dime.

Apparently, the allowance Meg gets is subject to rules the parents make and Meg wants more flexibility. Mother is trying to keep the peace. She wants to be fair.

MEG: And more to have in my savings.
MOTHER: I agree; I think she should have more. She should be able to spend more than ten cents on her sweets. What about letting her decide if she wants to spend the whole quarter or save part of it. Why should we say?
FATHER: The whole thing?

Father has no intention of being fair; he wants to be right. This is not a friendly discussion. They are discussing who is right and who has the right. Each one brings up his justification for his own point of view, instead of understanding the feelings of the others. The real issues are being cheated, being treated unfairly, not getting what you want, and feeling deprived. By father's remark he indicates how startled he is. It's unthinkable to him that Meg should decide for herself.

Mother, not interested in fighting, says:

MOTHER: Yes, let her spend the whole thing, whatever she wants. If we say she can only spend ten cents on sweets, then she wants a raise.

FATHER: OK, all right.

This is just like any labor dispute. The principals don't agree. Each one wants to get more, and neither sees an end unless one side gives in. Here both parents want to make the decision. It is not an effective agreement, because the children have not participated. The younger members have not had an equal opportunity to engage in a discussion that would lead to a solution.

MOTHER: What do you think about that, Meg? That's a sum you can spend. You would get a quarter and you can spend it all, or part of it, or save some of it.

MEG: And what about Glenn?

Meg is satisfied with the parents' decision, but wants to make sure that her brother also receives consideration. She also wants to hear the decision about her brother to make sure that he doesn't catch up to her. Father, in response, belittles his son and provokes him.

FATHER: That's up to Glenn. He's not interested. He'd rather sit there and eat his candy. We can ignore him.

GLENN: (whining) No-o-o-o!

MOTHER: What about your allowance?

GLENN: 25¢.

MOTHER: No, darling, we're not going to give you the same as Meg. You're younger, you get less.

FATHER: Do you want to be able to spend it all on sweets if you want? Without saving anything?

GLENN: Well, yes.

Although mother speaks in a friendly tone, the discussion is still heavily one-sided. She is trying to be democratic without knowing how to be. Both parents are unaware of how they take over. Mother now launches a lecture, full of explanations and condescension. The trouble is that although she says the allowance belongs wholly to the children, she does not trust them to learn how to handle it.

MOTHER: Daddy and I are willing to provide you with a bank, give you your allowance, and you can save part of it or spend it all.

GLENN: Spend it all.

MOTHER: No, that's up to you to decide. See, daddy and I buy you your clothes and your food and the things you need. But if you want other things, then you must save money so that you can buy these little things. We're not going to; we're not in a position to buy you these things, like these little cars that you buy or whatever. So if you don't save any money, you won't have it to buy these things.

When mother finishes her long explanation, which is really preaching, father is worried that the subject of money has not been thoroughly covered. The children have another source of income. He is concerned over who has the right to decide how that extra money is to be spent, and continues to fight for that right for himself.

FATHER: What about the extra money they get?
MEG: What about the big things we get?
MOTHER: I think we should establish that the big money . . .
FATHER: They can't spend more than their allowance on sweets.
MOTHER: Right.

For the parents, it's all decided. They have issued the order in autocratic fashion. But Meg is not satisifed.

MEG: What about the big things?
FATHER: Just a minute. So if you have a dollar or two dollars that you saved up from somebody else, or that grandma gave you, you can't spend that for candy.
MEG: But grandma said I can spend it on anything.
FATHER: But grandma is not your mother.
MOTHER: Grandma doesn't have to pay your dental bills. We do.
FATHER: All you can spend on candy every week is the 25¢ allowance.

The parents are still making the rules and announcing them. They feel threatened by the influence of grandma's money, and think of a reason why Meg should not spend it as she wishes.

This meeting continues as they discuss the relationship of sweets and cavities, and the work of the dentist; but throughout, both parents act as the fountains of wisdom. They announce their own point of view, instead of listening to each of the other persons. They sit in judgment making the decisions, instead of encouraging full participation.

They have a lot to learn—in company with most other families who are trying to make the shift from autocratic to democratic styles of living.

The significance of what has been pointed out here is that bringing in arbitrary solutions won't work in the long run. Children do not feel bound by decisions in which they have not shared, and will continue to use their energy to outwit their parents. The purpose of a free, open, friendly discussion is to allow each participant to express his own opinions that reflect his underlying feelings. This is in accordance with Chapter 8, "Coping with Conflict," in which the four parts of reaching agreement are described.

Each family, in the struggle to reach equality, has to learn its own themes and patterns; and each person needs to become alert to his or her own contributions to the family system. In some sessions, there may appear to be a solid equality; but at other times, there are signs that each individual is looking out for himself, shutting out the messages from the others.

The handling of money is a sensitive issue in most families. It is a difficult test of democratic parenthood for parents to allow children to learn on their own to deal with the problems money presents. The major purpose of an allowance for children is as an instrument for learning the management of money. If parents continue to issue instructions and to require accounting, the value of the independent experience is lost.

In the Jensen family, part of the agenda is the treasury report, but instead of hearing a report, the parents conduct an audit. They thereby intrude unnecessarily in the relationships between the children and hamper the management of individual funds. It can be seen that the parents feel justified in expecting a detailed report for every penny:

RUTH: For March, I paid up my church offering of $3.90 and I'm all paid up through April; spent 10¢ for a pack of gum; $1 for lunch money; 75¢ for a canoe trip; 50¢ for popcorn; and the Stantons paid me $5 even when they owed me $5.75, so they gypped me out of 75¢ for baby-sitting.

Father rises to the protection of his daughter, and seeks to right the wrong he feels she has suffered:

FATHER: Did you ever get it?
RUTH: The 75¢? No.
FATHER: Did you ever ask them?
RUTH: No. I'm just not going to them any more.
FATHER: Since they gypped you, you're not going there?
RUTH: No. They're not worth it.

He continues to question her ability to handle the situation:

FATHER: What are you going to say when they call you?
RUTH: I already did. They called me, and I said somebody already asked me. I should say something like "You have a lot of nerve"—something.
FATHER: No, you can do it tactfully.
RUTH: Dad, they should get the hint that they're cheap.

Here mother joins in, apparently satisfied that Ruth can cope:

MOTHER: Well, I think you've had enough experience with them not paying you right for too long.

RUTH: I owe Mrs. Weston for my Easter dress, $17; I owe Mom $20 for a down pay-
             ment on my skis; Fred owes me 40¢ for his golf bet.
FRED: No, I don't.

This begins a wrangle between the children in which father, trying to teach
money management, instead enables a quarrel over money to flare up:

RUTH: I gave Rhoda the $2 that I owed her, and all that's due me is 40¢ from Fred for
             the golf he played last year.
FRED: I already paid you.
RUTH: You only paid me $2. there's interest, remember?
FRED: I paid you off—you're not going to get any more. There's only 20¢ interest.
RUTH: But I never got that.
FRED: Well, you're not going to get it.
RUTH: It's doubled—it's a whole year, Fred. It's going to triple.
FATHER: You owed her $2 for a whole year?
FRED: I paid it, though.
FATHER: That's what the bank does. When they charge interest, if you don't pay it in a
             year, it's compounded.
FRED: Well, she'll never get it.

Father once again tries to be the judge of what's right, and to bring in
illustrations that are partial to Ruth. She is 17; Fred is 15; Rhoda, 11. Instead of allowing
Ruth and Fred to work out their differences privately without parental intervention, he has
created a dispute by bringing the financial transactions between siblings into the Family
Council.

Although the ostensible reason for teaching the children to charge interest is to
acquaint them with the operation of banks, the financial transaction is here a surface cover
for each one to win over the other. It's the "principle" of the debt as they speak about it,
but underneath it continues to be a question of who will win.

FATHER: Did you give her the $2?
RUTH: He gave me the $2 with no interest.
MOTHER: How much do you feel she should get?
FRED: Call the police!

Fred feels beaten already. His remark indicates that he feels hopeless and might
as well give up.

FATHER: The going interest rate in the bank is 8% on a loan.
RUTH: So that's—52 weeks in a year . . .
FATHER: That's 8% a year, so it's . . .

FRED: So I owe you 14¢.

FATHER: What's 8% of $2? That's 16¢—you said 20¢.

RUTH: But, see, I told him three months ago that it would double. I had told him 20¢, so it would be 40¢.

FRED: Yah, yah, oh yah, you're going to get 40¢.

Fred, having seen defeat coming, resorts to ridicule, the loser's weapon. He feels overpowered by his older sister, who has the help of the father, and this is probably a familiar situation for him. At this point the entire family talks at once as each one tries to assert his idea of what is right. The question is not what is right, but who wins. Ruth remains triumphant:

RUTH: This is a private business here—you should have gone to the bank. You have to go by my rules, because you could've gone to the bank. I'm not as liberal as the bank.

FRED: You're a crook.

RUTH: Well, then give me my money.

RHODA: She charged me 5¢ for a stick of gum.

This eldest daughter is used to having her own way, and will not be intimidated by pleas for justice or mercy. Her father, full of good intentions and eager to teach, cannot realize how he is deepening the conflict between his daughter and son.

Mother seeks a fair solution:

MOTHER: How much did you agree you would pay her as interest?

FRED: 20¢.

MOTHER: Then why don't you pay her the 20¢? Would that be acceptable, if he pays the 20¢ now?

The conflict is not about the 20¢; the conflict is about who will win—which of the two children will have his or her way. This can be seen when Ruth does not accept this reasonable suggestion:

RUTH: And 20¢ later.

Father, too, wants to arrive at a reasonable decision. But he does not see that his viewpoint will not necessarily prevail; even if it seems to be accepted, it cannot solve the underlying conflict, which is about Ruth's striving always to be ahead of Fred.

FATHER: Here's what we'll arrive at, Ruth. First of all, I think you learned a lesson not to lend any money.

RUTH: I'm not the bank.

FATHER: Ruth is right, because she can charge whatever interest she wants. That's the way the bank operates.

RUTH: I can charge 100% if I want.

FATHER: That's right, because some people can't get credit at the bank, so they go to the finance company that charges them much more interest.

Mother does not accept father's righteous support of his daughter, and continues to try to settle it her way:

MOTHER: What did you agree on when you borrowed from her?

RUTH: $2.20.

MOTHER: If that was the agreement, then go get her the 20¢.

RUTH: But that was a year ago.

FRED: It isn't a year yet—it'll be a year in June.

Again the family all talk at once, and it is clear that each member has a decision which he believes to be right. But none of them touches on the underlying conflict, which will erupt again and again in different forms. Although father and mother consider this problem solved, both Ruth and Fred find ways to avoid finishing it:

MOTHER: Do you want to get the money now and pay up?

FRED: I haven't got it.

Fred is really saying "No, I don't want to" to his mother, but finding other ways—ways that she doesn't accept:

MOTHER: You haven't got it?

FRED: I don't have any change.

RUTH: I'll take the $5.

MOTHER: She'll probably give you change.

RUTH: No, I wouldn't, because I want double, and after this week it's going to triple.

Ruth is really saying, "I don't want this settled. I need this debt to keep the fight going with my brother. I have to show him I can always win."

MOTHER: But you agreed on double . . .

RUTH: But he agreed to pay me the next week.

MOTHER: Well, OK, I suppose it would be all right.

RUTH: We discussed this at a couple of meetings, remember? Two months ago we talked about it . . .

Ruth acknowledges that she needs to keep this going. As long as her brother owes her the money, she has a way to show him his inferiority. He continues to fight her by refusing to pay up.

This time the parents put the pressure on, requiring Fred to go get the money to settle the matter. But no one is satisfied, because the underlying conflict never was expressed.

As soon as the quarrel erupted, the Family Council was disrupted and the bad feelings were intensified. Instead of helping the family members to learn to resolve their differences, this council meeting has divided the family into opposing factions, with winners and losers. The trouble with this situation is that losers usually try to get even.

How much simpler it would be for the parents to stay out of the disposition of individual finances, and let the members settle their affairs privately. This argument has solidified resentments between brother and sister. Although the money matter may be settled, the conflict continues.

When parents take a different attitude, problems move toward solution. For instance, when children bring up a complaint or a proposal, an effective democratic response is, "What do you think about it?" This will allow them to express their ideas and opinions, and the whole family can deal with the possibilities of solution.

When parents take the attitude that they are the sole sources of information and authority, the children are stifled and the conflicts continue.

It's not just a question of saying the "right" thing, but of admitting that no one person can possibly know all that is involved in any situation. Only by encouraging children to participate in the process can a council meeting be effective.

12

Universal Difficulties

Certain subjects arise again and again in every family. One of them is money and its management. As we have seen, the use of money presents situations in which both parents feel compelled to teach, to preach, and to lecture. Although parents think they are guiding their children, what they may be doing is covering up conflicts about other matters.

There is a better way to deal with money problems—a democratic way in which every family member is invited to contribute ideas and suggestions, and to discover limitations. As educators have proven, learning that comes about through active discovery is more effective and more lasting than learning that is assumed to follow receiving instruction.

One enthusiastic mother writes about the way her family approaches money problems, and how the Family Council has led them to this system:

> Whenever we take a trip, Jack likes to drive straight through. We leave early and keep driving until we reach our destination. Our finances are never so free that we can afford motel bills anyway, and he gives this as his reason.
>
> We were planning a trip to visit relatives. This drive usually takes twelve to fifteen hours. We had a new dog, and the kids and I thought it would be fun to take him along; but Jack was against it, with good reason. The dog was not housebroken, and would get carsick besides. We discussed our plans and tabled the trip until the next meeting.
>
> At the next meeting, we each came with a list of pros and cons, as we had agreed. The boys spoke of the discomfort of driving straight through, and said, "Other people stay at motels. Why can't we?" Jack said there was no way we could afford it. I couldn't argue about that, but thought of an example from *Children: The Challenge.* I said, "I'm willing to put up $10 out of the grocery money toward motels." Brad said he would put up $20, and Skip said he still had $7 birthday money to contribute. That made $37. Skip said, "Let's drive straight through on the way down and stay at a motel on the way back when we will be more tired." Jack couldn't refuse to stay at a motel after we had offered the money. I realized that it wasn't really the money, but his own determination to keep driving.

81

At that moment, Mrs. Stone discovered that the issue was not the money, but the conflict was over who would be boss. As long as her husband could use the excuse of insufficient funds, he could have his way regardless of the wishes or the comfort of his wife and sons. When the money was removed as a source of conflict, it became clear that the fight was really over domination.

> The next meeting we came with our lists of pros and cons on the dog, all except Jack. When it was his turn, after we had given our reasons for wanting to take the dog along, he said, "I feel so strongly about not taking the dog that I'm willing to pay the board for leaving it at the Vet for two weeks." Skip (then nine years old) said, "Isn't this interesting? He isn't willing to board the family so they can be comfortable on the trip, but he is willing to board the dog for his own convenience."
> Jack was shattered, and said, "Well, we'll take the dog, but you all know I'm against it. You'll have to take care of her—I'll have no part in it." Skip then said, "I'm learning all sorts of tricks today. All you have to do is be against something and then later you can give in without having to take any responsibility." Jack realized that this is typical of him, and said, "You're right. From now on, whatever we agree to do, we all share in the responsibility." This is what we do.

By trial and error, and continuing to hold meetings of their Family Council, this family discovered for themselves the four principles of conflict-solving described in Chapter 8: create mutual respect; pinpoint the issue; seek areas of agreement; and share responsibilities.

Mrs. Stone, in describing the effect of this meeting, says further:

> That trip set a precedent for us. We often all kick in money to do something we can't afford out of the family budget. We've had some great times. We decide in advance what we want to spend our money for, and often take a lunch or supper along so we can use our money for something special. Both boys have learned many skills in dealing with the real world: they can call motels to find out prices and alternatives, and get information from many sources. We all learned to camp, because we wanted to go to the seashore, but couldn't afford to rent a cottage. Family Council has made life much fuller for all of us.

In the Curtis family they have also learned the way to deal with money management so that the children learn without parents' preaching. The meeting that follows deals with the possibility of constructing a go-cart, and although the father is clearly not enthusiastic about the project, he manages to treat his sons' suggestions with respect and at no time throws cold water on their plans.

FATHER: Well, one item is piping. We could probably get it for about $5.
MIKE: That's what I said. That'll be the frame, then we need a steering wheel.
FATHER: But I don't want to start on it until . . .
MOTHER: What would happen if we decide to wait until we have enough money to buy all the parts, then start building the go-cart, but not until then. Otherwise what usually happens is that you buy $30 worth of wheels, or $60 worth, and it sits

around until there's enough money to buy the rest of the parts. Isn't that what usually happens?

Mother is showing her impatience, her hostility. She very obviously doesn't want a go-cart around the house, and is quick to bring up past projects. Her attitude sets herself up as an authority on what projects are necessary or advisable, and this isn't one she's going to approve. Father is not so hasty.

FATHER: Well, I could stop at one of these places and check out the prices and come back next meeting with the total amount.

MOTHER: I thought that was the arrangement at the last meeting.

FATHER: I came back with the price of the wheels. I don't know what a seat costs, or a steering wheel. The other things all have to be made.

MIKE: Well, the steering wheel we can buy at a store, like for a bike. You know those bike kind of steering wheels? That'd be good.

MOTHER: Well, what has to be done just to find out how much you need in terms of money to buy the necessary parts?

MIKE: Dad has to take me to about eighteen stores.

FATHER: We have to go around checking. We could do that next weekend.

MOTHER: I make a motion that we do that before we go ahead with any building.

Mother is so intent on blocking the project that she doesn't listen to father's plan. She only knows her own viewpoint, as is customary for most people. She knows what she wants to say, but this time she can't hear what the others are saying. They go on with their discussion, ignoring her motion.

MIKE: About how much does a lawn chair cost? Pete used a lawn chair for the seat on his.

FATHER: I don't know how much it would be.

ED: That's not what we want to use, though, dad. What do we want to use?

FATHER: They make a regular seat.

ED: Cross out lawn chair, if you put it on the list.

MOTHER: I'm not in favor of using our meeting time to decide on the parts we need.

MIKE: Oh yes, I am.

ED: I am.

FATHER: Well, the reason I brought it up is . . .

MIKE: Dad, what are we going to do about the go-cart?

FATHER: Next Saturday we'll take a ride and check the parts. Instead of going shopping and just wasting time riding the mini-bike and goofing around, we'll do something about the go-cart parts.

MOTHER: Well, then at the next meeting you'll bring back . . .

MIKE: Prices.

MOTHER: Prices on all the parts you need to put a go-cart together. If not all, at least the major portion.

Although mother keeps insisting on bringing the project to some decision point, father is determined to keep the entire subject open to possibilities.

FATHER: Why don't you look at the neighborhood ads, and see if you can find a go-cart. Like Ted said, there was one for $65 in his neighborhood that had everything.

ED: Then let's buy it.

FATHER: We still need the $65.

MIKE: That would be the cost of the wheels and frame, and then we'd have to go for the . . .

ED: I have an idea. I can . . .

MIKE: . . . steering wheel and the seat, and . . .

ED: We could get the $65 easy. Wait. With our . . .

MIKE: With our $30. How much would you be willing to put in, besides $30?

MOTHER: You have to find out how much it would cost. If three of you are saving money for it, one-third of the cost per person would be reasonable.

ED: Mom, could you kick in an extra balance, about $5?

MOTHER: An extra what?

ED: An extra balance. $5.

MOTHER: What?

ED: An extra amount of money. $5.

MOTHER: Oh, you mean you want me to contribute to the go-cart itself?

She demonstrates that she wasn't listening to anybody else, but merely concentrating on her own viewpoint. Her words suggest that the very idea that she should be asked to contribute is unthinkable.

ED: Yeah, just about—not you so much—just helping to get the $65 together.

MIKE: We only have, dad, now wait . . .

MOTHER: I don't know.

MIKE: We still need about $35.

ED: This bargain is pretty good, dad. What if we went there and it wasn't there any more?

FATHER: That's what I'm trying to say. We don't have the money. That's how the whole subject came up. We don't have a system of saving money for when we need something.

Instead of preaching to his sons that they should save their money instead of squandering it, father includes himself as an equal with them, and speaks of a tough problem that they can help to solve. He doesn't scold them, or belittle them for wanting something they can't afford, but presents a problem they can all discuss together.

MIKE: Well, Ed and I have started. Again.

MOTHER: What I was—I brought it up with dad. What I was trying to say . . .

Mother is on her own trail, still not paying attention to how the discussion is moving. She wants to tell them the right way to do things.

MIKE: Not dad. The money in our banks is for that. Now I have an idea. After we open our banks, why don't we take the money and put it somewhere?

MOTHER: Like in your savings account?

MIKE: No, I have a better idea. Why don't we take the money out of my bank, and instead of saving, whenever we have extra quarters or anything, we'll put it in the other bank.

ED: I have no money.

MIKE: I have a dollar bill there, Ed. And then when we open it up, and there's twenty-some dollars in there, we put it in the black bank. When the black bank has $50 in it . . .

ED: Dad, can you give me a dollar bill?

MIKE: Then we take the money from the black bank and go buy the frame and the steering wheel and the . . .

MOTHER: But you don't know how much any of these things costs.

MIKE: We'll estimate. Right now.

MOTHER: Yes.

MIKE: $50 is $10 away from the wheels.

FATHER: Let's table it until Saturday, when we can check prices.

This time father has defused the argument, because he can see that mother wants to squelch the whole idea. He holds firm to the plan to get actual prices, and then figure them up. He has another reason:

FATHER: I like the idea of building one together rather than buying one because then we'll have all the fun of building it.

ED: I don't want to build one like Sam's. You saw that one.

FATHER: But it works.

ED: Yeah, but still. I want to build one that . . .

MOTHER: Yeah, but at least he has one and you don't.

Here mother's hostility comes through. Not only has she continued to interrupt and to try to spoil the plans the others are making, but she chooses to deride her son. This is disrespectful to him and to the concept of the Family Council. Father alone maintained a democratic attitude. He encouraged each one to speak, he listened to them all, and made comments which showed a spirit of friendliness and openness.

Another source of difficulty in every family is the distribution of the work in the household. As we have seen in Chapter 9, the democratic way to get the work done is to view it is the responsibility of everyone. This is hard to do as long as family members continue to think of the jobs as mother's, or father's, and to feel that the others are merely helping out.

Sharing responsibilities requires that each person understands that the whole family depends on him to perform the task he has undertaken; that he does it to the best of his ability and is not criticized if he fails to reach perfection. Sharing means that no job is more valued than any other. As soon as the menial work is degraded, the person who does it also feels put down.

Those jobs nobody wants are best left undone, so that everyone can see whether or not they are really necessary. Often a parent—usually mother—continues to feel responsible, and goes over the work doing what others left undone, or doing over the work that a young person failed to do perfectly. A classic example of this is bedmaking. A child leaves his bed in the style he prefers. After he leaves for school, mother goes into his room, remakes his bed, and straightens it up to be neat. There is no chance that this child will ever learn to take care of his own things as long as he knows that his mother will follow up.

In one family, a list of chores is posted on the refrigerator. Right after the meeting of the Family Council, family members sign for the jobs they choose to do. Since it is understood that all the chores must be done, "There's a mad rush to get the easiest ones," the mother reports. Freedom of choice is one of the strongest forces to push family members into action.

Depending on the age of the children and on the other conditions in the family, there is some work they cannot perform alone. This does not mean that an adult must take over. An atmosphere of cooperation developed in the Family Council and in day-to-day living shows up in the cooperation required to do such work.

The Fallon family show us how they go about it. Bert and Laura have five children: Chuck, 11; Joan and Jane, twins, 9; Dale, a daughter, 8; and Kevin, 4½. Joan, Jane, and Dale share a room, and of course it gets messed up and needs to be cleaned.

JOAN: I was thinking. I wondered if we could keep our room clean, this week and next week, then maybe we could move our beds around.

DALE: And we could try to keep our room clean for about five weeks.

MOTHER: I think it's been pretty good, Dale. It's been better, don't you think? I think so. You can have your friends in and stuff. I don't think it's been bad. While we're talking about changing the beds around, can I bring up something else about the same subject?

DALE: OK.

MOTHER: You know, sometimes each person takes his own week. Does that work out all right for you? Do you like it that way?

JANE: I don't like it that way.

MOTHER: No, you don't. Well, what do you think? Do you have a better idea? What do you think about that?

DALE: One day we—one time we had our own parts, by our beds, to pick up everything of ours, and we had to put away everything that was on the floor by our part, even if it wasn't ours.

MOTHER: How did that work?
            (Giggles)

MOTHER: Well, what do you think? Do you want to go back to that way again?

ALL: Yes.

MOTHER: Or do you want to work it out yourselves? Whatever you think. We can talk about it now, or do whatever you think.

JOAN: I want to talk about it by ourselves. I think we could figure it out.

MOTHER: OK, why don't you try it for next week? One more idea I did want to suggest. Is it OK if I do it now? I was thinking: sometimes each person takes her week, and does it. But the harder parts—the closet, the high shelves, the dressers, and the windowsills, all that stuff—it takes a lot of extra time, and it really doesn't have to be done every week. I was thinking—since it involves scrubbing and different things like that—how would it be if for three weeks you work it out how you want to do it, the way you've been doing it or all three together or whatever? Then on the fourth week, I would help you; and that's the time we would change your beds around, maybe straighten the drawers, and you would tell me what clothes need mending, and change the books, or whatever needs to be done. How does that sound? Would you like me to help you one time a month or not? What do you think?

JANE: I don't really think I like it.

DALE: Well, if we each had our week, you'd have to help the first one, wouldn't you?

MOTHER: No, I'd just help you the fourth time, after you all three did a turn; and then we all four would do it together on the fourth week.

FATHER: What would be the purpose of your helping them?

MOTHER: Because some of the scrubbing—it's very hard to scrub the baseboards with the three beds and two dressers in the room, and they do like to change their beds around often. I have to do that part on my own anyway, and I figure it's easier for me to do it when they have already cleaned up and the beds are moved out. Once a month, it's just part of regular housecleaning that I do. So what do you think?

JOAN: I think it's a good way.

MOTHER: All right. Why don't we try it? Why don't we start next week? That'll be the week that I'll help you, and we'll get it all settled, and then after that you can talk about it and decide how you want to do the rest.

Throughout the discussion, mother has continued to accept her daughters' responsibility for those parts of the work they can do, and her own responsibility for the more difficult parts. The spirit of cooperation is in every message exchanged.

There will always be lapses in job performance, and mothers may become irritated. Mrs. Gordon brings up her dissatisfaction:

MOTHER: I have something to say about jobs. I think that, you know, daddy hasn't been home lately; it seems that when daddy's not home our whole family order is not the same. It's kind of half-baked.

GAIL: I don't have anything to do except the scraping, which can be done in one second in the morning.

MOTHER: Then I guess I'm really talking to you, David.

FATHER: You don't think it's your job to pitch in on everything?

DAVID: Well, sometimes we go to a restaurant.

MOTHER: I'm not talking about when we go to a restaurant. I'm talking about when we're home. It seems that when daddy goes out of town for a few days and we're home it's kind of like, you know, you come down and eat and leave, and there are just a few dishes, and you forget to look on the list. You know, the rule is, it doesn't matter, somebody else can pitch in. That's fine, but I don't want to be the one who does the pitching in all the time all by myself. I think I may have to start just leaving things around. It's too much work for me to do all by myself.

Mother has fallen into the trap. She sounds like a typical "good mother" who doesn't get any help with her hard work. They are not treating the family work as responsibilities to be shared, but as chores to be performed to assist mother. And she, instead of taking action, is threatening. She expresses hostility toward her husband for being away from home, causing the family order to fall apart. Actually she need only refrain from doing some of her share in order for her children to catch on. Instead, she threatens for "next time" and the children know very well that it is only a threat.

DAVID: Well, you can remind us.

MOTHER: I don't think I should remind you. I think you're capable of remembering yourself.

DAVID: Sometimes we forget, so you could remind us.

MOTHER: No.

DAVID: You can't?

MOTHER: No.

DAVID: Why can't you?

MOTHER: Because I think it's your job to remember what your jobs are. Who reminds me?

DAVID: Well, we remind you, so why can't you remind us?

MOTHER: I don't think it's necessary to talk to you about things like that. I think you're old enough and responsible enough to remind yourself. If you really want to remind yourself, you'll do it.

What mother forgets is that he won't remember as long as she is willing to do what needs to be done. The only way David, or any other child, will learn is through the consequences of the incident. What he has learned is that it doesn't really matter whether or not he does what he's agreed to do. Mother will always "pitch in." His asking to be reminded is just another way of asking for service from her. She refuses to render the service of reminding, but goes on rendering the service of performing his work.

13

Approaching Equality

Equality is the ideal toward which we strive. It's very difficult to attain and, like other ideals, is elusive. Once in a while it appears, bringing with it harmony and the solution to many vexing problems; but for the most part we struggle in our families to reach it.

In our work with families, we are continually impressed by the changes that family members can make, and the gains that follow. Over a period of time, families that hold a Family Council find that democracy grows as autocracy shrinks. There will still be times when old habits emerge, but as family members learn the ways of democratic living they also learn how to cope with the eruptions of old patterns.

We sought an example of an ideal Family Council meeting to present to the readers of this book. As we searched, we realized that the ideal doesn't exist. We present the transcript of a meeting that was to deal with the potentially explosive subject of a private television set for two boys. This family is certainly moving toward democracy and equality:

MOTHER: Do you have anything you want to discuss?
MIKE: Yeah, the TV upstairs.
FATHER: That's a good subject. It seems that we acquired a TV set before we really had a chance to discuss it, so I feel that we should start to discuss it with the question of "Should the boys have a TV set in their room?"
ED: Yeah, why not?
FATHER: In the past, I was against having a TV set upstairs for a few reasons. I'll present my reasons, and then we can go on from there. We have the TV set now, and there's not much we can do about that. It was a gift, so we have it. The reason I wasn't in favor of it is that I didn't like the idea of the boys spending all their time in their room watching TV and not being members of the family.

91

MIKE: Now, wait a minute. Most of the time we're watching TV it's after our bedtime hour, or early morning, and you're not up; you know, sometimes during the day we watch TV up there, but not very often.

MOTHER: Despite the fact that it's never been discussed, we haven't had any real problem about it.

FATHER: Wait. You haven't even given me a chance. I'm not saying I don't want it . . . I said this is the reason I had for not wanting it. It was that if they had a TV upstairs, the boys would feel compelled to go upstairs and to watch the TV up there and never be members of the family; while I feel that TV watching should be a family thing. We all watch a program together.

MOTHER: OK.

FATHER: I didn't want this to happen. It hasn't happened. I'm glad it hasn't. But this is the reason I was against it. Now that we've had that TV set for about a week, it hasn't proven to be a big problem, and I feel that if the boys are willing to set up some sort of rules and regulations so that we know . . .

ED: We know that it's our job to turn it off; it's our job to—if we're not watching it, turn it off—to make sure we don't stay up too late watching it, and not have it too loud, and stuff like that. We don't leave it on.

FATHER: My biggest concern would be that you would leave the TV set on all night. That was my biggest concern.

MOTHER: Yes, especially if we weren't home.

ED: Well, it hasn't happened yet.

MOTHER: Right. So far there haven't been any problems. You've handled it really well. It's been a pleasure to have it.

ED: It probably won't happen either.

MOTHER: Mike, did you have anything you wanted to bring up about the TV?

MIKE: I wanted to know if when you buy the *TV Guide* you could buy two of them, one for the downstairs TV and one for the upstairs TV.

MOTHER: That's a good consideration, because last week we lost our *TV Guide*.

ED: But what if she doesn't buy the *TV Guide*?

MOTHER: Something happened to come in the mail about *TV Guide*, and here it is. Take a look at it and see what you think. If you fellas send for that and pay for that, you get a *TV Guide* that costs you, I think, 25¢ if you buy it in the store—or maybe it's 15¢ in the store. I'm not really certain. But if you buy a newspaper to get a TV guide, it costs 20¢. If you buy a *TV Guide* in the grocery store, it costs 15¢. If you send for it by that method, it's less than 11¢ apiece. Plus, if you send for it that way, the copy comes mailed to your home each week, so you don't have to go out to the store to get it.

MIKE: Ed and I could do that; that's not so much.

ED: Is that all we have to pay for this thing? $3.00 we'd be paying, and then at the bottom here in small print, it says, "Please send me the next 56 weeks of *TV Guide* for only $5.88 after," and so on and so forth and to wit.

MOTHER:	You know the $2.98 price is not for a whole year.
MIKE:	Yeah, I know; 28 weeks. That would be—56 is the whole year.
MOTHER:	Right. A little better than a year.
MIKE:	That would be $6.00.
MOTHER:	Right. Do you think you two could afford to scrape together $3.00 apiece to mail in for *TV Guide*?
MIKE:	Yep. I could do it.
ED:	How long does this last just for our $3.00?
MOTHER:	One year. You get 56 issues.
MIKE:	Offer expires when?
MOTHER:	Well, it expires one year from the date that you order it.
ED:	No, what I mean is, how soon do you start sending in the money?
FATHER:	You only send it in once.
MOTHER:	You have to send it in just once.
ED:	No, what I mean is, say you got this yesterday, when's the deadline?
MOTHER:	Oh, I see what you mean.
MIKE:	It doesn't say a deadline.
MOTHER:	I guess there is no deadline.
MIKE:	We'd get our own *TV Guide* for only $3.00 for a whole year, Ed.
FATHER:	Is it cheaper to do that than to use the newspaper?
MOTHER:	Yes, because the newspaper is 20¢ a copy.
FATHER:	Yes, but we have a newspaper delivered every day.
MOTHER:	But there isn't a TV guide in that paper. It's only in the Saturday paper, and that's . . .
FATHER:	There's a TV section in the paper.
ED:	But I don't like to go fishing for a TV section.
MOTHER:	In the Saturday paper there's the TV guide that we use for ourselves, downstairs.
FATHER:	This one here?
MOTHER:	No, the one that comes in the paper.
FATHER:	No, I'm talking about the daily newspaper. It has a pictorial, and a theater, and a radio, and a TV section.
MOTHER:	Oh, I see what you mean.
FATHER:	I'm telling you. If they were willing to use that, they could save themselves some money.
MOTHER:	That's right. I hadn't even thought about that. You know, the TV listings for the day are in the newspaper every day.
MIKE:	Yeah, but . . .
FATHER:	Well, $3.00 apiece doesn't sound like a lot of money; except you have to come up with it all at one time.
MOTHER:	Yes. And then they'd have to get a money order.
FATHER:	No, I'll be glad to furnish them with a check if they give me the money.

MOTHER: OK. What are you figuring, Mike, the cost per issue?

FATHER: He's figuring what it would cost at 15¢.

MIKE: It would be $8.40. We'd be saving more than $2.00.

MOTHER: Well, it's up to you.

MIKE: It's not a lot, but if you keep it going year after year, you could save yourself a lot.

MOTHER: I don't think so, because this is a trial offer, so it's cheaper. So the next time we would renew this it would be different. I think it would cost more.

MIKE: Maybe.

FATHER: I'm reading it. If you take 28 . . .

MOTHER: It would be helpful to know what a *TV Guide* costs in the store.

FATHER: . . . issues for $2.98 on a trial basis, if you don't like it, and you don't feel you want it any longer, you can stop.

MIKE: Yeah, why don't we take a trial?

ED: Why don't we get it for 20¢ with the paper?

MOTHER: Because this is only 11¢.

FATHER: If you were going to buy another paper, it'd be 20¢, but if you'd read the newspaper that comes every day . . .

ED: No, I wouldn't like that, because you don't buy me my own newspaper, and all that. And it's even hard enough for me to find the sports section in it, or page number two, or stuff like that.

MIKE: Well, Ed and I are going to split together and count the money and send it in.

MOTHER: Is that agreeable to you, Ed?

ED: Yeah.

FATHER: You boys want to take the 28 issues on a trial basis, then, so if you don't like it you can find another way.

MOTHER: That sounds fine to me.

FATHER: There's nothing to stop them from using the family's TV guide; but if they take it upstairs, then it doesn't do anybody any good.

ED: As long as we bring it down.

MOTHER: That was what happened the first week. Not only did they take it upstairs, but it got lost. So nobody had a TV guide that week, including us. They expressed a desire to have one of their own; that was why I saved that thing. It came with the newspaper or something—I don't remember how we got it.

FATHER: I would like to bring up another thing about the TV set. Being an old set, it could break down at any time.

MIKE: So don't be disappointed if it does.

FATHER: If it does break down, I just want you boys to understand that I don't feel impelled to fix it, or to pay to fix it.

MIKE: Well, you know how we had such a clear picture when we first got it? Now there's a little bit of a ghost.

FATHER: Well, that can't be helped. We even have a ghost on the big set.

MIKE: Yeah, but the big set's been going so long—it's years.

FATHER: I'm just saying that if this set breaks down . . .

MOTHER: Your set is just as old.

FATHER: It's going to have to be fixed.

MIKE: It's our job to fix it.

FATHER: It's your set, so the money will have to come from you boys as far as I'm concerned.

MIKE: Yeah, like . . .

MOTHER: Maybe not . . .

MIKE: How much would you ask for?

MOTHER: It depends on how much it would cost.

MIKE: How much would it cost?

MOTHER: Maybe not all of it. Maybe we would prorate it on the basis of what the repair job costs.

MIKE: How much would it cost to pay the repair bill?

MOTHER: It's cheaper if you have a portable unit, because if you carry it into the shop instead of having a service man come to your house . . .

ED: That costs more money.

MOTHER: Right. You won't have to pay for a service call, for a man to come to the house.

MIKE: Do you get charged for the gas he uses, and his car and everything?

FATHER: This is probably another reason that it would be a good idea not to leave it on overnight.

MIKE: If it overheats or something, there goes the TV.

FATHER: If it breaks down, you would have expenses.

MIKE: You wouldn't be paying them.

FATHER: I don't choose to, because you know how I feel about the TV anyway.

MOTHER: Well, we'll have to cross that bridge when we come to it.

MIKE: If it ever comes.

MOTHER: Right. The set could go for a long time, or it could break down next week. You never know with TVs.

MIKE: You never know with other things, either.

MOTHER: That's true.

MIKE: But this is a good TV. It's not a cheap one like that other one we had. It's a good brand.

MOTHER: That reminds me. How about Jim? Does he do repairs, or does he just work in the office in the plant?

FATHER: They sell the TVs, but he might be able to do us some good. I don't know.

MOTHER: Maybe he would know a good service outfit around here that services that brand.

MIKE: Or if he didn't, he could get the list.

MOTHER: That's true. Other than that, I don't see any potential problems with having the set up there. I think the boys are happy with it, and it hasn't really hindered any of the good times we've had as a family.

FATHER:	That's what I was concerned about. I thought that when the boys came home from school they would be upstairs and we wouldn't see them until suppertime, and then they'd go back upstairs, but I'm glad . . .
ED:	We haven't done that one day.
FATHER:	I'm glad to see that they did come down, and that they joined us if we were watching TV.
MOTHER:	And the boys do have a good point, because there are times when we have a meeting or something. It's really early for them to go upstairs with nothing to do, when they ordinarily might be watching a TV show.
FATHER:	Yes, so maybe it's a good thing it happened the way it did. Maybe if we had discussed it before we got it, we might not have gotten it. Since we got it spontaneously, the problem solved itself.
MIKE:	Sure, because grandma said, "You better take care of that TV."
FATHER:	Well, that's all I have to say on the subject.
MOTHER:	Do you have anything more, Ed?
ED:	Ummm.
MOTHER:	Daddy said he would be willing to issue a check if you came up with cash, so whenever you come up with it daddy will write a check for it.
MIKE:	Oh, I can come up with it.
MOTHER:	OK. Do you have anything else?
ED:	I think I can come up with a dollar right now.
FATHER:	It doesn't have to be this minute.
MOTHER:	Is there anything else, Mike?
MIKE:	No, I don't think so.
MOTHER:	Then do I have a motion for adjournment?
MIKE:	I move the meeting be adjourned.
ED:	I second it.
MOTHER:	OK, then the meeting is adjourned.

The entire meeting lasted about twenty minutes, and dealt with only one question. It can be seen that this family has learned the art of friendly discussion. The parents gave no orders, the children made no demands. The unexpected acquisition of a television set could lead to parents giving orders, children crying for privileges, and a whole set of family conflicts about it. In the Curtis family, whom we have met before on these pages, they handled the problem in a calm way while still making their opinions known to one another.

It may be that the script of this meeting made dull reading, in comparison to other more lively sections. That is the point of including it here. When a family has learned to live with the Family Council, conflict is minimal, fights are fewer, and the meeting proceeds in an atmosphere of calm.

This is part of the process through which a family moves toward harmony through democracy using the Family Council.

14

Questions Parents Ask—and Answers

This book has been written at the request of parents who want to use the Family Council to help them have a more harmonious family life. We have tried to cover every aspect of the what, why, when, where, who, and how. However, you may still have questions to which you have not yet found answers.

For that reason we have compiled in this chapter some of the questions we are most frequently asked, with our answers. As you will notice, they deal with the routine aspects of family life, for families can deal with a crisis more successfully than they can take care of the daily annoyances. The problem of who is to take out the garbage, which occurs daily, often presents more difficulty than an imminent danger. In the face of a challenge from outside, the family can quickly unite and deal with it.

Our questions and answers may not fully satisfy your need to know, for this section must necessarily deal with generalities that apply in all families. A thorough knowledge of the principles of Adlerian psychology will provide the basis from which you can deal with your unique situation. If you wish, you may regard this chapter as a review or as a test to see how well you have mastered the concepts of equality as practiced in a Family Council. As you read each question, try to anticipate the answer. If, when you read the answer, the subject still isn't clear, refer to the chapter where it is dealt with more fully.

Finally, knowledge comes only through practice. Understanding can only follow experience. To learn more about how the Family Council works, put it to work and watch what happens.

QUESTIONS PARENTS ASK will be found under the following headings:

Who	Difficulties
Age: how old	Results
Time: how long	Evaluation
Content	Rewards

Who

Is the Family Council only for families with problems?

Family Council was first conceived in family counseling when parents came to Family Education Centers to learn how to get along with their children. It was suggested as a way to begin to treat children more democratically.

Because it worked so well to help alleviate conflict between parents and children, it has been adopted and refined by many families that have only the routine problems that occur in daily living.

The idea is widespread that parents and children have to be in opposing camps, that their outlook is bound to be so different as to produce continuous conflict. Despite mounting evidence that autocratic rule no longer works, many parents still try to rule their children by giving orders, making decisions, punishing and threatening punishment.

We believe that competition destroys human relationships and that human beings flourish in a spirit of cooperation. Therefore, every family can reach its potential, and the potential of its individual members, through the use of a Family Council.

Does every family need a Family Council?

No, but every family can profit from making a Family Council part of its life. In families in which there are conflicts, in which relationships are disturbed, or in which communication is disrupted, a Family Council can help improve the situation.

Would it be possible for a husband and wife to hold a Family Council together before there are children, or before the children are old enough to participate?

This is a possibility that has not yet been tested, but there is no reason why it would not be effective. In most marriages one partner is more outspoken than the other. One partner is accustomed to being dominated by the other. Even in man-woman relationships that are not legally binding, this will be the case. One partner tells the other what to do either overtly or in a disguised manner.

If the two partners want to achieve a more equal status with a view toward reaching cooperative sharing, it would be an excellent idea to begin to hold regular meetings at a time set aside for the purpose of working out mutual concerns. The meetings would be an opportunity to practice accurate listening, honest verbal communication, and a thorough examination of the distribution of responsibility.[1]

In this way, when children join the family, an aura of equality will have already been established, and a democratic family life-style will develop.

My husband (or wife) does not want a Family Council. Should I try it anyway?

If there is one more person in the family with whom you can meet, do so. If you are willing to be open, to listen, to treat others as equals, and not to be the boss, go

---

1. See R.J. Corsini, "The Marriage Conference," *Marriage Counseling Quarterly 5* (1970): 21–29.

ahead and hold the meetings. If one person in the family changes his or her way of reacting to situations, the climate of the family changes and the way is open for further change. It is important, however, that the spouse who chooses not to join be treated with respect. No good can be accomplished if the Family Council is used to get revenge against the person who chooses to stay out. Decisions can be made, however, that exclude that person.

I am a single parent, with an only child. Can I have a Family Council?

Again, yes. Look at the Family Council as an exercise in learning equality. When there are only two people involved, the chances are great that one will take supremacy over the other. Sometimes it is the parent who gives the orders, but just as often it is the child who has that parent trained to do what he (the child) wants.

Do we hold the Family Council if visitors are present?

If visitors are present, all family members decide together whether to hold the meeting as scheduled or to delay it for another time. We would strongly recommend holding the meeting as usual. It is a good way to let others see what a Family Council is and how it works, and your guests will probably be interested. Their participation is to be encouraged if they are staying with the family more than a day or two.

Age

How old do children have to be before the family can hold a Family Council?

There is no minimum age, but in order for meetings to be fruitful, at least one child should have reached the stage of verbal communication. Until the oldest child can put his ideas into words, the children cannot participate in a Family Council. However, when there are other children in the family, even an infant can be brought to the council meeting to listen and to observe.

Can you start a Family Council when the children are already into their teens, and even partly independent?

Certainly. This is the time in the lives of young people when they need to become independent from parents. It is an ideal time to learn the processes of democratic living. At this age it is also likely that children have a great deal to contribute to discussion of the family situations, and have habits and plans that may put a strain on the entire family. The Family Council is a good place to work out the cooperation to help everybody to be satisfied.

Time

How long should a meeting be? How do you tell if it's long enough?

There is no one prescription for the length of a meeting. More importantly, no one person is to decide what the length should be. The length of time the family spends together in the meeting is at the discretion of the entire group. Probably the important thing to remember is that a parent should not attempt to prolong the meeting when others have lost interest. This is the kind of question that the entire group can tackle as one of its first matters of business. When there is discussion about ground rules, the time of the meeting and what day it is to be held, the group can decide on a length of time.

Content

How do you decide what is an appropriate problem to bring up?

Only if you honestly mean to let the family group propose a solution, and if you are willing to try that solution, should you bring the problem up. If a parent brings up a problem in the hope that the children will be sympathetic and see his or her point of view, it won't work.

What are some of the things that can be taken up?

Anything that concerns the family as a whole. For example:

Family fun: games, parties, picnics, vacations

Family relationships: rules, regulations, procedures

Family work: jobs, projects, chores, assistance, outside work

Finances: expenses, allowances, gifts, purchases

Problems: conflicts, difficulties

Plans: job changes, house changes, visitors, education, community participation

What should not be taken up at the Family Council meetings?

Anything between the parents which they wish to keep private. For example: marital disagreements; sexual conflicts; differences of opinion on religion, politics, or relatives.

How can we handle finances in the Family Council?

As the business of the entire family. For the children in a family to understand the nature of financial support, parents need to disclose how the money comes in and how it goes out. As much as possible according to the ages and sophistication of the children, parents can discuss the family financial goals and accept the suggestions and contributions of the children. For instance, when an extravagant request is made, a parent may offer a minimal amount of money he or she feels he can contribute, and then put it to the group to figure out how to cover the balance.

When a problem comes up at a meeting, is it necessary to insist that a solution be found at that meeting?

On the contrary, it's probably impossible. As soon as anyone insists, the democratic atmosphere is lost. That person has set himself up as the authority who decides what must be done. The solution must emerge from participation of all the family members present at the meeting, or it's no solution.

The best solutions are reached when everyone in the family is feeling the effects of a situation. Each member, parent and child, is then ready to listen, to respect, and to consider all the possible solutions that anyone else suggests. It's a basic mistake to push for an immediate solution.

You may expect and assume that a solution will be reached, but demands will get you nowhere. If the solution is not forthcoming, the subject should be tabled for a week.

What if it's necessary to find an answer right away?

The only kind of problem that can't be tabled is in the category of "the house is on fire"—and for that you don't need a meeting. If something comes up at a meeting that you can't reach agreement about, you just don't. You acknowledge that "*we* can't reach agreement"—not "you children won't listen" or "you won't cooperate." Simply acknowledge that "*we're* not ready to solve this one."

What can parents do to encourage children to participate?

Remember the basic concepts of equality and democracy, and discard the autocratic position. Listen more than talk. Think more than shout. Specifically, here are some examples:

1. *Provide a treat at the end of the meeting.*
2. *Include pleasant news or pleasant plans.*
3. *Follow through on decisions.*
4. *Don't scold between sessions.*
5. *Discuss things calmly.*
6. *Stand up for your ideas, but don't insist.*
7. *Go along with what seem to be mistakes, after expressing your position clearly.*
8. *In the face of persistent sabotage, leave the meeting.*
9. *Beware of surface agreement. Don't say you agree, even with your spouse, if you really don't.*

Do we really need rules and officers and a set time and written records?

Yes, in order to maintain order, to prevent fights, and to ensure participation. Unless there is at least a skeleton system that everybody understands, there may be chaos.

Difficulties

*How do parents sometimes contribute to the sabotage of the Family
Council?*

Unknowingly, even well-intentioned parents can make mistakes that cause the
Family Council to be unpleasant and unsuccessful. Some common ones are:
1. *Talk too long.*
2. *Criticize.*
3. *Say too much.*
4. *Procrastinate.*
5. *Act bossy.*
6. *Skip a meeting.*
7. *Forget to follow through.*

All of these are errors parents often make. Watch out for them. Remember to
be an equal participant, and don't do anything you wouldn't want the others to do. As a
parent, you will be setting an example of conduct, and if you "pull rank," the others will
rebel against you.

What if nobody else is interested in my problem?

You can't force others to be concerned with your anxiety, but you can take
action that will bring others into the problem. Or, you can ponder your own purpose in
being annoyed, and maybe understand why the others are not interested. It may be that you
have to postpone consideration of that problem for a later time.

What can a parent do if the children start a fight during the Family Council?

If the parent is chairman, call the meeting to order. If the fight continues, ask
the rest of the members if they want to adjourn the meeting. Or it may be better as
chairman to say or do nothing, and wait for the fight to be over. Under no circumstances
assert your authority as a parent and try to settle the quarrel by making a judgment. Remain
an equal participant and you may find the other members will handle it.

The same principles apply if a child interrupts, makes disrupting noises, or acts
silly. If a parent is the chairman, a request for order is appropriate. If the chairman is
someone else, let that person handle the disturbance. If the disruption is unbearable, you
may leave; the Family Council is voluntary for everyone.

What if one family member refuses to come to the first meeting?

Hold the Family Council anyway, with other family members. It is important
that the absence of any one member not become an issue for the others. It is essential to be
working toward cooperation rather than warfare, and it is risky to threaten the absent
member with the impact of the decisions of the Family Council.

How do you know what you can let a child do?

You can't always be sure. Usually the younger a child is the more responsibility he will want to assume, and parents are faced with the problem of deciding whether to let a child undertake what might be too difficult a job.

In this case, one of the parents must take the time to be available for instruction and supervision so that the child can try to perform that task. If he does not, this is not to be regarded as a failure, but merely as a job to be postponed until he is bigger or stronger.

The principle to follow is that if a child volunteers for something, you encourage him to try, unless it is clearly beyond him or dangerous for him. Many parents have been astounded at the things their children can do in time of crisis. Those same powers are available at other times. They only need to be exercised. Perfection should not be expected. Nobody can do a job perfectly the first time, or maybe ever. Although a parent can perform it better because of many years of practice, there is no reason to deny a child the opportunity to try.

How do you handle family members who come to the meeting only prepared to deal with their own problems?

Through the routine operation of the Family Council, the person with a one-track mind will become aware that others have problems too, and that others have valuable contributions to make to everyone. The constraints of living together as a family make it advisable for each family member to consider the rights and feelings of the others. In the Family Council, because of the concentrated attempt to work together, the self-centered person begins to acknowledge the existence of others, and the needs of others.

Results

What if a decision is made at the Family Council and not carried out?

This means that not everyone agreed with the decision. Some may have just gone along with a more dominant person, or even with the majority, just to get the problem over with. Anyone who doesn't carry out his share in the following week merely didn't agree to do it. Lip service was given, and that's all.

The only thing you can do is to take the appropriate action that suits this behavior, and then bring the subject up again at the following meeting.

For appropriate action, read *Children: The Challenge* to learn about the effects of natural consequences and logical consequences.

One lapse doesn't mean that the Family Council meeting was a failure. What it means is that all family members are not yet tuned in to the themes of equality and democracy.

How can a parent help make the Family Council work?

Mainly, by following the guidelines we have given and watching out for the pitfalls. Some of the assertive ways you can reinforce the Family Council are:

1. *Support and follow through on family decisions.*
2. *Refuse to make decisions outside the Family Council that belong on its agenda.*
3. *Consider all relevant problems and subjects for discussion, even when they concern an absent member.*
4. *Participate as an equal with other members of the family.*

Can the Family Council really change a family?

What can change is the relationships among the people in the family. An authoritarian parent who usually gives orders can learn in the Family Council to listen rather than demand, and to carry this habit over into daily living. Similarly, a child who never speaks up can learn in the Family Council that others do listen to him, and thus acquire the courage to express his ideas at other times.

Most valuable is the opportunity to solve conflicts. When family members know that there is a place to bring up their difficulties and a way to get them solved, they are less likely to exaggerate the importance of those difficulties.

How long do we keep decisions?

Until they are rescinded. Changes in plans or decisions are to be brought up at the next meeting, and all family members present at that meeting asked to reconsider. No one family member may arbitrarily change a council decision. Each member is responsible for his own actions as a result of that decision.

Evaluation

Is there any way we can evaluate the success of our Family Council meetings?

In order to make an evaluation, you have to know what the goals of the Family Council are. In general, the goals of the Family Council are to improve the relationships among family members and to help the family to function more effectively. The criterion for evaluation would then be whether any particular meeting has contributed toward reaching those goals. Basic criteria are listed in Chapter 3.

There is a pitfall in evaluating meetings, however. If a parent is too concerned about doing things the "right" way, the danger is that he will not do them at all. Many families give up too soon because they feel they have not achieved their purpose in starting a Family Council.

The total purpose is to maintain the democratic atmosphere of equality, of mutual respect, and of sharing responsibilities. This cannot be achieved in a few meetings. As long as members of the family are sharing a household, regular meetings will contribute to the achievement of harmony and efficiency.

What is the most important element for a successful Family Council?

An understanding by the parents that they are to operate in the spirit of total equality in the Family Council. They are not to act as supreme authorities; neither are they to act in a condescending manner. Father and mother need to become aware of how difficult it is to give up authority and to function as equals.

Just as parents have difficulty in giving up authority, children find it hard to believe that they are to be treated as equals, and may attempt to place the parents in an autocratic position.

Rewards

What can we hope to gain from Family Council as individuals?

There are great benefits to be earned in understanding the job of being a parent. It is possible to achieve a better relationship with your children, to communicate with them more effectively, and to solve mutual problems.

There is also great gain for each person who participates, child as well as adult. You learn how to listen to other people and to their problems and how to cooperate in finding a solution. You learn how to look beyond an expressed conflict toward what is really going on between and among people. You learn how to make plans that will work because everyone who is to participate has had a part in making those plans. You learn how to share responsibilities rather than give orders or take commands.

In short, in the Family Council a person can learn to be a socially responsible, cooperative human being.

Does Family Council enable an individual to handle his own problems?

When you learn to express yourself in a family group, it becomes easier for you to express yourself with other persons outside the family without having to fight or to compete. You acquire confidence in your ability to cooperate and are thus enabled to cope with the stresses of daily living that arise outside the family.

Bibliography

For Parents:

Books

Marguerite and Willard Beecher, *Beyond Success and Failure* (Julian, 1966).

——. *Parents on the Run* (Julian, 1955).

Don Dinkmeyer and Gary D. McKay, *Raising a Responsible Child* (Simon & Schuster, 1973).

Fitzhugh Dodson, *How to Parent* (Signet, 1971).

Rudolf Dreikurs, *Adult-Child Relations* (University of Oregon Press, 1961).

——. *The Challenge of Child Training* (Hawthorn, 1972).

——. *Children: The Challenge* (Duell, Sloan, 1964).

Rudolf Dreikurs and Loren Grey, *A Parents' Guide to Child Discipline* (Hawthorn, 1970).

Loren Grey, *Discipline without Tyranny* (Hawthorn, 1972).

Articles

Rudolf Dreikurs, "Raising Children in a Democracy," *The Humanist*, vol. 18, no. 2, 1958, pp. 77–83.

For Teachers:

Books:

Don Dinkmeyer, *Child Development: The Emerging Self* (Prentice-Hall, 1965).

——. *Developmental Counseling and Guidance* (McGraw-Hill, 1970).

Don Dinkmeyer and Rudolf Dreikurs, *Encouraging Children to Learn* (Prentice-Hall, 1963).

Rudolf Dreikurs, *Child Guidance and Education* (Alfred Adler Institute, Chicago, 1973).

——. *Psychology in the Classroom* (Harper & Row, 1968).

Rudolf Dreikurs et al., *Maintaining Sanity in the Classroom* (Harper & Row, 1971).

Arthur G. Nikelly, *Techniques for Behavior Change* (Thomas, 1971).

Oskar Spiel, *Discipline without Punishment* (Faber, London, 1962).

Articles:

Rudolf Dreikurs, "The Cultural Implications of Reward and Punishment," *International Journal of Social Psychiatry,* vol. IV, no. 3, Winter 1958, pp. 171–178.

———. "Coping with the Child's Problems in the Classroom," in *Professional School Psychology,* edited by Monroe G. Gottsegen and Gloria B. Gottsegen (Grune & Stratton, 1960).

For Everybody:

Books:

Alfred Adler, *The Science of Living* (Anchor, 1969).

———. *Understanding Human Nature* (Fawcett, 1961).

———. *What Life Should Mean to You* (Capricorn, 1958).

Heinz L. Ansbacher and Rowena Ansbacher, *The Individual Psychology of Alfred Adler* (Basic, 1956).

Rudolf Dreikurs, *The Challenge of Marriage* (Duell, Sloan, 1946).

———. *Fundamentals of Adlerian Psychology* (Greenberg, 1950).

———. *Social Equality* (Regnery, 1971).

Articles:

Rudolf Dreikurs, "The War between the Generations," *The British Journal of Social Psychiatry*, vol. 4, no. 1, 1970.

Rudolf Dreikurs and Marvin Chernoff, "Parents and Teachers: Friends or Enemies?" *Education*, vol. 91, Nov.-Dec.,1970, pp. 147–154.

Pamphlets:

Rudolf Dreikurs and Margaret Goldman, *ABC's of Guiding the Child* (Family Education Association, Chicago, 1967).

Rudolf Dreikurs and Vicki Soltz, *Your Child and Discipline* (National Education Association, Washington, D.C.).

Index

2 3 4 5 6 7 ← P Y → 9 8 7 6 5 4